CHASING
MIRACLES

CHASING
MIRACLES

The CROWLEY FAMILY
JOURNEY *of* STRENGTH,
HOPE, *and* JOY

JOHN F. CROWLEY

with Ken Kurson

Newmarket Press
New York

This book is published simultaneously in the United States of America and in Canada. All rights reserved. This book may not be reproduced, in whole or in part, in any form, without written permission. Inquiries should be e-mailed to permissions@newmarketpress.com or write to Permissions Department, Newmarket Press, 18 East 48th Street, New York, NY 10017, FAX (212) 832-3629.

This book is published in the United States of America.

First Edition

Library of Congress Cataloging-in-Publication
Data Available Upon Request

ISBN 978-1-55704-910-0

Quantity Purchases
Companies, professional groups, clubs, and other organizations may qualify for special terms when ordering quantities of this title. For information, e-mail sales@newmarketpress.com or write to Special Sales, Newmarket Press, 18 East 48th Street, New York, NY 10017; call (212) 832-3575 ext. 19 or 1-800-669-3903; fax (212) 832-3629.

Manufactured in the United States of America.

www.newmarketpress.com

MAKE·(A·)WISH.

A portion of the proceeds from this book will be donated to the Make-A-Wish Foundation.

*This book is dedicated to my children.
To John Jr., who has my life;
Megan, who has my soul;
and Patrick, who has my heart.
And to their mother and my wife, Aileen,
who shares my life, heart, and soul
in every way imaginable.*

Contents

FOREWORD

Many people over the years have asked us how we first met and when and where our first date was. John always jumps to answer ahead of me, and takes great pride in telling people that "she asked me out." As if he were some prized object of desire by the girls at my high school, the all-girls Academy of the Holy Angels, which was a few towns over from Oradell, New Jersey, where John attended the all-boys Bergen Catholic High School. I quickly remind people that while it is true that I did the asking, John—who was known to study quite a bit back then—remarkably had no social plans that weekend. We finished as high school sweethearts and married two months after I graduated college in 1990. Life has been pretty normal ever since…. *not*.

Through the long journey of our now more than twenty-five years together as a couple, we have learned much from many people in our lives. And we have learned a great deal from each other as we have grown together.

I was sixteen when John and I went on that first date to the Holy Angels winter formal. In February

2008, I was preparing to turn forty years old—a long way past high school and the ever more distant memories of that winter dance. We believe that life should be celebrated whenever possible, and there is no better way to celebrate than with family and close friends. So my daughter Megan and I came up with the idea of a Cinderella-like ball, complete with ball gowns for the ladies and tuxedos for the gentlemen. Much of the night was a spoof, like my rhinestone tiara with the gaudy "40" dangling from the crown. It was a way to celebrate a unique spirit of family.

The party was an unspoken milestone not for me, but for our two youngest kids, Megan and Patrick. Diagnosed in 1998 with a rare form of muscular dystrophy known as Pompe disease, they weren't supposed to see their mom turn thirty, let alone forty. But the party wasn't melodramatic; it wasn't nostalgic. It was just plain old fun. And it was filled with laughter and love.

This book is filled with that same laughter and love, told through many stories and vignettes. Some will make you cry. Many more will make you laugh out loud. This book is not meant solely for parents of special needs children or families struggling through health issues. The stories and lessons that John presents here are lessons for us all. Perhaps even more than any of our contributions to Pompe disease research, it is these learnings in life—from our failures as much as our successes—that will be an enduring legacy for the Crowley family.

For years, John has spoken in public about our family's unique journey to find a treatment for Megan and Patrick's disease, and much has been written about that effort, including a wonderful book by Pulitzer Prize–winning journalist Geeta Anand called *The Cure* (which was the inspiration for the feature film *Extraordinary Measures*, starring Brendan Fraser, Harrison Ford, and Keri Russell). My husband has a special gift of eloquence to articulate thoughts, feelings, and perspectives. John's speeches, however, do not focus on the events between the kids' diagnosis and the eventual life-saving enzyme replacement therapy that he helped to develop. Instead, they reflect on the lessons in life that we as a family have learned throughout this journey. They represent the fabric of who we are. And that is what this book is all about, building on the many inspirational talks that John has given over the past few years. This book is our family's attempt, as told through John's writing, to share much of what we have learned. What follows is not an accounting of events so much as a showing of ideas, ideas about how to live life.

There are many people who have influenced us through the years, and many of the lessons from those people are told here. It is from our three children that we have learned the most, however, without their ever knowing that they have been teaching us along the way. John Jr., Megan, and Patrick have taught us more about life and love than we have ever taught them. Each of our children's paths has been different, each marked by their own personalities, strengths, frailties, and dreams. They each have special "needs," but they also have special "gifts." We are thankful for each new day and we believe we have much to share. This book is one way of sharing our lives.

—Aileen Crowley,
December 2009

INTRODUCTION

I was just shy of eight years old when my dad died. In his obituary, the Englewood Chief of Police said that everyone loved my dad and that he was a cop's cop and a Marine's Marine. I remember his sense of humor and I remember him looking exactly like I look today. His dark Irish genes continue on.

I was born April 7, 1967, in Englewood, New Jersey. My mom and dad had known each other for all of a year or so. Some friend had arranged for them to meet, and their first date was at a bar in Englewood called O'Prandy's. They hit it off famously.

My mother, Barbara, still likes to tell the story of the first time she took my dad home to meet her very Italian parents, Frank and Jeanette Valentino. My dad was excited because he loved Italian food. But my mother wasn't quite sure how her parents would react to an Irish cop. They'd never had an Irish guy over to the house before, so instead of spaghetti with her legendary sausage sauce and wine, my grandmother served corned beef and cabbage and steak and potatoes, and actually had a six-pack of beer ready for him. My mom says he was never so disappointed.

We lived in a little apartment in Tryon Gardens in Englewood, half a mile or so from St. Cecelia's Church. I always remember it as this great big apartment complex, but when I go back today to reminisce, I see that it's only a couple of modest courtyards surrounded by all these little garden apartments. But it was an incredibly warm, loving place to spend my childhood because Tryon Gardens was basically a Crowley and Valentino family compound. Think frontier settlement for Irish Catholic cops and Italian carpenters.

My mother's father, Grandpa Frank, was the superintendent, so he and my grandmother lived there for free and received a little stipend each month for maintaining the property and the apartments. My dad's brother, Jim, also a cop in town, lived there with his wife, my Aunt Marie and their two kids, Jimmy and Laura, as did my mother's sister, my Aunt Michele, and my dad's only sister, Aunt Cappi, with her kids.

So growing up, it was kind of neat to have all my cousins running around. We would only have to look out the window to wave to each other every day. My grandfather took care of a couple of other apartment buildings to make ends meet, including the ones that replaced the Palisades Amusement Park in Fort Lee. When I was little, he would take me on his maintenance calls all day long while my mom and dad worked. I wore my baseball cap, and he built me a little toolbox. He put a couple of small tools in there, but he'd always put a book or two and some snacks in there as well. Over the years, he'd put in fewer tools and more books. I'd want to do the carpentry with him, and he did teach me how to hammer nails and fix a few basic household items. But he saw that I wasn't all that good at carpentry and, more important, he didn't want me to work with my hands for a living.

My grandfather had only a seventh-grade education and could barely read, but he drilled into me the importance of getting an education. My parents and my other grandparents pressed me to study hard, insisting that a solid academic education was the only way to get ahead. Nobody in my family had ever gone to college. Growing up, I don't think I even knew anybody who had gone to college. But even as a boy, I knew I wanted to go.

My mom more than anyone would remind me to study, work hard, and move forward in life. She dreamed of my attending the best college possible. For her, even the Ivy League wouldn't be too far a stretch for her oldest son. And on the Crowley side, college was important but the Ivy League was less impressive than the dream of a Notre Dame degree with a Crowley name affixed prominently to it. The Irish would have it no other way. How great to have a kid in South Bend one day, they frequently mused.

On my first day of kindergarten, my dad drove me to school in his police cruiser. When we arrived, I flicked on the lights and blew the siren. It was awesome.

My dad's mother, Catherine Crowley, died in Englewood Hospital right around then. They didn't let kids in the room toward the end, so I'd wait outside while my dad visited with her. I remember looking through the window and seeing this very sweet lady about to die in her fifties from diabetic complications. My grandfather, John, who had spent his whole life working a very tough job in a rubber factory, retired after her death and would die himself the following year. Then my dad died six months later. In less than two years, in the Crowley family both parents and their eldest son had passed away.

My dad died on January 12, 1975, on duty. A flaw in the exhaust of his police cruiser allowed carbon monoxide to seep into the car and he was poisoned accidentally. I had never been to a wake before. I saw my dad in the casket. He was wearing his crisp police uniform and had the Marine Corps honor guard flanking his casket at the front, in deference to his prior service with the Second Force Recon Unit of the Marines. There were hundreds of people there, and I remember overhearing two secretaries from the Police Department saying, "Just awful, tragic, John was such a great guy, and so young, so young." My dad died three days after turning thirty-five. Overhearing these ladies at the wake, I remember thinking, "Hmm. Do they not know that he wasn't all *that* young? He was over thirty-five." Ah, how our perspective about "old age" changes as we advance through life.

At the funeral, the huge area of worship at St. Cecelia's was filled and people lined the streets outside. Even the news media were there. We sat up front, and

I remember the priest talking directly to us during part of the Mass. My brother Joe was too young to go to the funeral, so the priest directed his remarks to me. He told me that God's will is difficult to understand and that sometimes you have to grow up sooner than you thought. He said I'd have to step up and help out in ways I probably hadn't expected. That was really the first time that I began to realize my dad was dead and wouldn't be coming back.

At the end of the ceremony, my mom decided not to take me to the gravesite. It was bitterly cold, and she also thought that the hole in the ground and the twenty-one-gun salute might prove a little too much for me. The last thing I remember from that day is my dad's casket with the flag on top being placed into the hearse as I was being driven in the other direction.

My dad had always been in control. He didn't lose his cool. Even when his job as a police officer in our hometown presented problems. Even though he wasn't a tall man, he seemed ten feet tall to me. Part of it was the way he carried himself, part of it was the uniform and the badge, but there was something else as well: a sense of purpose.

Anyone who reads the names of the first responders murdered on September 11, 2001, can tell by the last names that an outsized share of those heroes were the Irish and Italian Catholics who are drawn to professions like firefighter and police officer. My dad believed that he had been put on this earth not as a random collection of atoms and cells and genes and chromosomes, but to protect his country and neighbors and family.

Aileen and I met at a Halloween party. None of my friends from Bergen Catholic had any money, and we were excited to go to this giant house in Franklin Lakes because we figured the girls would have some dough. Cute Catholic school girls with money—it didn't get any better than that. We went to the party in full costume. One friend was a hobo and another was a baby; I was dressed as a priest. Aileen was the only one not wearing a costume because she was way too cool. It was 1984, and she was wearing a pink polo oxford with the collar up and a plaid skirt and penny loafers with a shiny penny tucked in each one. And those piercing green eyes.

About six weeks later there was that winter cotillion at Holy Angels—yes, the one to which *she* asked me out! I'd seen Aileen once or twice since the Halloween party, but we had still barely spoken. My friend Jordan asked me, "Hey, you remember Aileen? She's looking for a date to the winter formal. Tommy says she's gonna call you and ask you." Sweet. But she called when I wasn't home and my mother reported, "Some girl 'Eye-leen' called you." I said, "Oh no, it's 'A-leen.'" So I called her back and said, "Hey, A-leen, it's John Crowley." Aileen replied, "Eye-leen." People to this day call her A-leen because of the way it's spelled, the same way her grandmother spelled it.

She began to say, "Hey, there's this dance..." and I jumped in and said, "I'd love to go." Our first kiss was a month later. It was January 1985, and we were watching the James Bond movie *The Spy Who Loved Me* on the Betamax in my basement. The movie ended and we just looked at each other and kissed on the couch. It was just a short, sweet little kiss. It wasn't a big make-out session. It's really hard to make out to Carly Simon singing "Nobody Does it Better." A tad boastful, I thought. But it lit the fire.

I attended the U.S. Naval Academy and largely put myself through Georgetown University, Notre Dame Law School, and Harvard Business School. Mom and Grandpa were right: education could open a whole new life for someone, no matter how modest their family roots. But sometimes life doesn't unfold the way it's supposed to. I was supposed to be an executive at a big corporation when I "grew up." My beautiful wife, Aileen, was supposed to be a carefree mom. Our first child, John Jr., was born in December 1994. In 1998, our next two children were supposed to be dead.

When we were told our two youngest children both had Pompe disease and had just months to live, we decided to survive their fatal diagnosis. We needed to beat nature and beat time. We needed to learn a lot about this disease in a hurry. And we needed to learn a lot about ourselves as well.

Today, the Crowley home is a boisterous, happy place where wheelchairs zoom through the halls and our two Jack Russell dogs try to stay a step ahead of our three happy children. When one of the kids asks Aileen or me why our family isn't exactly like some other family, our stock reply can be relied on: "Well, that's why they're making a movie about our lives!"

The reality is that, for all that makes us unique, the Crowley family is exactly like every other family in America. We want what's best for our children, our neighbors, and our future.

The specific challenges our family faces may be rare. But the ways in which we've tackled them—the strategies and methods we've used to cope and to conquer and to live—have provided lessons that I hope will inspire any family.

In 1998, when John Jr. was a little more than three years old, Megan and Patrick were diagnosed with Pompe disease, a rare and fatal neuromuscular disorder. We had never heard the word *Pompe* (pronounced "pom-PAY") until that Friday, March 13th, when a neurologist in Oakland, California, told us that our fifteen-month-old Megan had the disease and that she would not live past her early childhood. And he told us that we needed to get our then seven-day-old Patrick tested as soon as possible because there was a 25 percent chance that he would have the disease as well, which was confirmed four months later. From that day in March, that word, that disease, would forever redefine our lives. It changed us before we could change it.

Aileen and I are both recessive carriers of a gene that is involved in the production of an enzyme that breaks down sugar in the muscles stored as glycogen. People who don't have Pompe produce this enzyme, and their glycogen is broken down and converted into energy for their muscles. Aileen and I, being silent carriers of this genetic defect, had no history of the disease in our families.

In the span of about a day we went through the shock, grief, anger, and denial that come with such a diagnosis. But within the span of that same day, we together also reached one other emotion that would define our journey with Megan and Patrick: determination. We had no idea if we could change the course of their disease, but we didn't want to look back years or decades from then and wish we had done something else, something more for them—and for all those who loved them.

And so we reached out to every doctor and researcher around the world who knew anything about this horrible disease. We raised money from family and friends for nonprofit charities to drive science toward a cure for Pompe.

As the kids' disease slowly ravaged their bodies, we grew increasingly frustrated with the pace and direction of the research. And so we took a risk, a big risk. In March 2000, I left the security of my marketing job with a large pharmaceutical company and partnered with a researcher to start a tiny biotechnology company, Novazyme Pharmaceuticals, focused on developing a treatment for Pompe. Aileen devoted herself as the mother and all-encompassing caregiver of three children.

What our fledgling start-up company lacked in money and experience, we made up for in passion, hard work, and commitment. We built that tiny biotech firm over an eighteen-month period into a 120-person business and sold it to Genzyme, one of the world's largest biotech companies. As part of that larger company, after many twists and turns and the efforts of hundreds of people, we finally discovered and produced a medicine to treat Pompe disease. The kids got their "special medicine" on January 9, 2003. Megan was six years old and Patrick was four years old. The medicine saved their lives by reversing the life-threatening enlargement of their hearts. For a time, the medicine even greatly improved their muscle strength.

Today, Megan and Patrick are in the seventh and sixth grades, respectively, at John Witherspoon public school in Princeton, New Jersey. Their special needs, older brother, John, is in the eighth grade there. Megan and Patrick are still profoundly affected by their Pompe disease—they will never walk and they remain on ventilators. But their hearts are fixed. They are alive, smart, and happy. I currently serve as President and CEO of Amicus Therapeutics, where I continue to work with some of the greatest physicians and researchers in the world to develop potentially newer and better medicines that can help

Megan and Patrick and many others like them who suffer from genetic diseases. Aileen still has the hardest job of all taking amazingly good care of the kids—and of me.

In many ways, we are an average American family, and this book describes how we dealt with a very serious set of challenges. We did for our kids what almost any other parents would have wanted to do: first, help them survive; next, help them thrive. Our outcome was ultimately successful because of a lot of factors: hard work, determination, love, faith, and, yes, some degree of luck. Along the way, our hardships and failures have been at least as plentiful as our joys and successes. We are at peace now with our life. We are thankful for all we have and for each new day with our kids. And we are still amazed at times that so many people refer to our lives with our kids as a "story." To us, it's not a story. It's everyday life.

This book consists of what the past eleven years have taught the Crowleys about family, faith, life, and love. After we had accepted our children's diagnosis and were determined to fight it, Aileen and I struggled to maintain our marriage within the confines of a constant state of emergency. For several years I would travel the world to launch my start-up and raise funds for a cure for Pompe. I'd return each week to a home filled with chaos: whirring and beeping machines, the occasional wildly incompetent nurse, all in a house never designed for two children attached to 40-pound ventilators.

And throughout these years, we slowly began to enjoy a real marriage again, apart from the children, and even began having dates again. Real dates, too—dinner, nice clothes, and wine, away from the house. Megan and Patrick need someone responsible and knowledgeable with them twenty-four hours a day. If their ventilator tube were to slip out while they were sleeping, they would die. They are such fragile little kiddos. A couple of months ago, on our way out to a date night—I had my sport coat on and Aileen was dressed beautifully in a little black dress—a new night nurse had fumbled handling an emergency with the kids. A few years ago, I might have fired the nurse on the spot, and resigned myself to a few hours of self-pity. Now, I said, "So be it. We'll have our date in the hallway." Aileen ordered a pizza, I set a small table with a white tablecloth, and we ate pepperoni pizza outside Megan's bedroom, still dressed in our best. We opened a bottle of wine and listened to some quiet music. We listened, also, to the rhythmic sounds of our Megan and Patrick breathing. Just breathing. It was as beautiful a date as we've ever had.

Our lives have settled into a routine that seems wholly normal to us. Occasionally, I get painful flashes of what life might have been. I was in Portland, Oregon, in April 2009 watching the filming of *Extraordinary Measures*, the movie that was inspired by our family. It was an incredible experience: Harrison Ford's trailer among dozens lining the street outside the massive warehouse that contained the soundstages,

24

hundreds of extras re-creating scenes from our recent past, an amusement park shut down for the day to reenact extraordinary events from our somewhat ordinary lives. The film crew built an exact replica of Megan's gigantic, 300-pound wheelchair; the only difference is that it's got a hole in the seat so the actress Meredith Droeger, portraying my daughter, can stand in it. They didn't want her to lose circulation from sitting for hours at a time. Also, since Megan's legs are completely immobile, they didn't want the camera to record an accidental twitch or movement. I watched them film a long scene, then the actress playing Megan jumped up to stretch her legs. I had to look away. It was so very bittersweet.

Over the past few years, Aileen and I have tried to reflect on the meaning of all this and what lessons we have learned from this incredible journey. That's what this book is about. It is our effort to convey to others the perspectives we have drawn from all the experiences in our life—not from our "story." We hope that others can be inspired and learn and live a better life from all that our family has witnessed, lived, and come to understand. It's a life full of strength, hope, and joy.

Part I

STRENGTH

CHAPTER 1

TRUST AND FAITH

*M*y *baby girl was three years old. She had her hair in pigtails. She was sitting on the edge of her bed. This was back when she had enough strength to sit up on the edge of the bed. At the time, I was really struggling with "trust" in my business. Trusting the science. Trusting the financing. Trusting the system. Trusting in myself.*

I was sitting on the floor next to the bed and reading Megan her Princess book, and I said, "Megan, you've got to be careful, sweetie. You're too close to the edge, and I don't want you to fall. But if you do fall, you know that Daddy will catch you."

Megan just looked down at me. Without saying a word, she smiled, closed her eyes, stretched out her arms, and allowed herself to fall forward.

I caught her and held on. Then I asked her why in the world she would do such a thing. With little muscle control and a body whose every system was already deeply compromised by the ravages of her disease, a headfirst fall like that on a hardwood floor could have been disastrous. And then I saw that she was laughing, looking me right in the eyes. She knew exactly what she had done. She had fallen on purpose and dared me to catch her.

She knew that I would. I said I'd catch her, and I did. Ever since, I've always wondered why she did that. Was it to experience the thrill of free fall? Or maybe to show me in her own special way that she trusted me completely, without a moment of reservation?

Late at night, July 2009. Princeton, New Jersey.

Aileen and I are lying in bed and we get on the subject of falling in love. The two big news stories of the day were about a governor who was going to try to fall back in love with his wife and about the breakup of the couple from the reality TV series *Jon & Kate Plus 8*.

Aileen and I joke about an idea that is undoubtedly repeated in homes across America: "If they really want to do a reality show that would entertain people, they ought to film us every day." At the Crowley house, the kids zoom around in their wheelchairs, the nurses and therapists come and go twenty-four hours a day, the medicine flows, the dogs bark and run. Throw in our brothers, cousins, and many friends and you've got yourself a reality show. Maybe even our own network (thanks, but no thanks!). Our conversation quickly turns to couples and how they fall in love in the first place.

Aileen asks me, "When exactly did you fall in love with me?"

I reply, "Honestly, there wasn't one particular moment that I can remember. I think it just evolved."

After our first kiss, I didn't tell Aileen "I love you" or anything, and I didn't go to bed thinking, "Gosh, I love this girl." But I did have strong feelings even after just the first few dates. And by St. Patrick's Day, I knew for sure that this was the girl I was going to marry. It didn't take long.

Now, in Princeton twenty-four years later, I tell Aileen this and ask her, "Okay, your turn. When did you know?"

Aileen says, "Do you remember when we went into New York?"

At first, I'm not sure what she's talking about. Then I think about it and say, "You know what? I do remember. Did we go in with a bunch of guys and girls back in high school?"

Aileen says, "Yes. It was in December, the weekend after that first winter dance. Even before our first kiss. A group of us went into the city to check out the Christmas tree at Rockefeller Center and had lunch at Friday's, and you sat next to me on the bus on the way back home. It was awful traffic getting out of New York and you kind of fell asleep in your seat. We went through the tunnel and your buddy said jokingly, 'John, the driver needs money for the toll.' You were half asleep and you took a dollar from your pocket and in a semi-conscious state handed it up to the driver. You never hesitated. That's when I knew."

The commitment of marriage is greater than any commitment in life. Over the years, Aileen and I have had our share of difficult times. After Megan and Patrick were diagnosed with Pompe disease, we struggled to find a rhythm that would work for our family. We hadn't envisioned a future together being dominated by a disease we had never heard of, by the daily threat to our children's lives, by the constant need for care and demand on resources.

We began to understand in time, though, what mattered most to us. All those things that had drawn us to each other were still there. They were even more deeply seated. Together, we had goals, history, the sort of telepathy that married couples develop over time. We shared a purpose in life. Somehow, we reached a level of maturity where we began to think of our lives together not as a sprint but as a marathon, where the tough patches were not bitter failures but hurdles to overcome.

It occurred to me that night, chatting in bed twenty-four years after we met, and more in love with my wife than ever, that what family really is about is trust.

Without ever saying it out loud or discussing it, Aileen and I developed a couple of rules, each based on an implicit reliance upon and trust in each other. First, when one of us is in a tough spot or a bad mood or slipping into feeling sorry for ourselves, we give it a couple of hours and no longer than that. Second, we are not both allowed to have a sad moment at the same time. In our situation, we just kind of wordlessly realized that if both of us were struggling simultaneously, the whole house would come apart.

That's what I'm getting at when I describe trust as the key element of marriage. Of course it refers to the obvious elements of honesty and fidelity. There's a subtler form of trust at work as well: the knowledge that someone will be there to pick you up when you can't be strong. There's also trust that your partner is going to provide for the family in ways you never could—a division of labor, of sorts.

Much of our early stressful times together just after the kids were diagnosed were exacerbated by key differences in our approach to life. Learning to see those differences as wonderful, valuable enhancements to our family has saved our marriage.

I got it through my head that Aileen is never going to be a person who puts together a spreadsheet of all the nurses' schedules and maps them against the children's activities and then sits down to reconcile all the insurance statements and bills. That's just not who she is. When it comes to actually taking care of the kids, the house, and being the glue that keeps not just our family but our extended family together, however, Aileen is without peer. She is the music around our house every day.

"God's Work Must Truly Be Our Own"

Our family has derived strength from placing faith in one another and in God.

In my spiritual life, I have tried never to ask God for specific intervention, as in "God, please let the Phillies win tonight," or "God, please make this clinical trial work well." I don't have a sense that God intervenes so directly in the world and I don't believe in predetermined fate, either.

But I do agree with what John F. Kennedy said at the end of his inaugural address: "With a good conscience our only sure reward, with history the final judge of our deeds, let us go forth to lead the land we love, asking His blessing and His help, but knowing that here on earth God's work must truly be our own."

When I pray, I try to focus in two directions. I give thanks for life and everything that I've got. And I pray for the people I love to have strength and inspiration in their lives. I pray for my kids: that they're happy, that they're at peace, that God gives them grace. But I don't ever pray, "God, from heaven reach down with your hand and manipulate those cells and allow the enzyme to be as active as it can be and thus reach its target." Instead, what I do pray for is that God will give *us* strength and inspiration and share His hope and His grace with me so that I can give it to others as they work to develop these treatments and cures. I think that's how God works through each of us to create miracles.

In my personal life, there have been times when I've been very devout in my faith and times when I've been a lot more skeptical and questioned its role. Like a million Irish and Italian kids growing up in New Jersey, I learned the basics of Catholicism early. When I was very young, my family was what you'd call "holiday Catholics": Christmas, Easter, weddings, and funerals. After my dad died, my mother enrolled me in CCD (Confraternity of Christian Doctrine) class at St. John's Church in Bergenfield. I still have the shiny gold CCD book and I remember the teacher would say things like, "Jesus loves you; now let's all draw a rainbow and a picture of your family."

For my first communion, my mother allowed her Italian roots to bloom. She dressed me in a blue velvet tuxedo with the biggest bowtie imaginable and shiny white patent leather shoes. Apparently, the number and depth of your ruffles made you a better Catholic. All my relatives showed up and we went to a little restaurant afterward. This being 1975, my mom hired a long-haired guy to come by and strum a guitar. He closed with "Bye, Bye, Miss American Pie." I thought it was awesome.

After we moved to the nearby town of Norwood a year later, we started to attend Mass more regularly at Immaculate Conception Church. That was really the first time that church, and a church community, connected with me on a deeper level. The parish priest, Father Ken Moore, made quite an impression on me. He was a Carmelite priest—he wore the long robes and all—and had taught at Notre Dame, so he was very educated and fluent in five languages. He spoke in this heavy Irish brogue and was such an impressive and thoughtful guy. I was in fourth grade and we had just moved to a new town, and I was really missing my dad. Father Ken was a magnificent role model—and a paradigm of what a priest should be.

Father Ken's brother, Father Tim Moore, was the parish priest at St. Cecelia's in Englewood. Father Tim's claim to fame, in addition to being a terrific priest himself, was that in the 1940s he had hired a new football coach at St. Cecelia's, a young fellow named Vince Lombardi. It was Lombardi's first coaching job, and he remained very close to the Moore brothers throughout his legendary career. He even made Father Ken the team chaplain of the Green Bay Packers. You can see Father Ken in his robes pacing the sidelines next to Coach Lombardi on clips of the first and second Super Bowls.

Father Ken developed a friendship with Wellington Mara, the longtime owner of the New York Giants. He eventually became the Giants team chaplain and he'd get them to hold a charity fundraiser for the church every year. Father Ken was beloved by the Giants players and coaches, Catholic or not, and they were very respectful. About thirty New York Giants would show up for a fundraiser at our church each year—greats like Phil Simms, Lawrence Taylor, and Phil McConkey. I remember Gary Jeter, who was this enormous defensive lineman. He had hands the size of tennis rackets. He picked me up with one hand and hoisted me into the air and said, "Man, you're a little dude." I said, "Wow, you're a big dude!" He was a gentle giant. Several times, I got to go with Father Ken to Giants Stadium to say Mass in the locker room before practice and games. It was exciting for a kid to be growing up on the periphery of the New York Giants.

I had started to be involved in the church, and it had become a very social aspect of my life. But much more than that, a light had switched on. A priest with a very human touch taught me the true meaning of faith. Without being cognizant of it, I somehow went from belonging to a church and a church community to suddenly praying hard and trying to be more thoughtful about faith and thinking about why we are here and what our purpose is. Sometimes I'd find myself getting to school ten minutes early and I would sit there quietly and pray during the 7:00 a.m. Mass. "God, I need help," I would say. "Would you help me? Would you give me strength?"

At Mass one day, the bulletins included an announcement that said, "We're recruiting this year for new altar boys." After Mass I went up to my mom and told her I wanted to be an altar boy. There was a deacon, Jim Pullati, a younger guy with a family, who did all the training. My biggest fear wasn't getting up in front of the crowd or carrying the cross. My mom had instilled a healthy dose of fear in us that dissuaded us from playing with matches as children—something like "If you touch a match, you'll burn the house and yourself. If the fire doesn't kill you, I will." It worked. Before Mass, the altar boy had to light all the candles. I didn't know how to light a match. My mom actually bought me a little Bic lighter and I would go around and light the candles with it. Once I had the logistics of altar-boying down, I was ready to roll.

What I was getting from religion then is exactly what I get from religion today: strength, inspiration, and a special sense of purpose. My dad dying unexpectedly had shaken me. I thought of all the people who went to bed one night feeling some measure of peace in their lives, only to wake up to a day that would change that feeling forever. Maybe it's a diagnosis about one of their kids, a car accident, a loved one passing on, a lost job, a fire. At some point in our lives it happens to every one of us, sometimes more than once. It is the ultimate question that has bedeviled mankind for eternity: Why would a loving God allow bad things to happen here on Earth? I don't know. But I do know that faith in God, something greater than ourselves, is an important part of our lives in the Crowley family. It has given us strength when we so very much needed it. And I pray, too, that Saint Theresa is right: "God is even kinder than you think."

People ask me all the time how long we think Megan and Patrick are going to live. The truth is, we just don't know. They've already lived a lot longer than they were expected to. They may live many more decades. If they were gone tomorrow, we'd of course be incredibly sad. There'd be an emptiness forever. But I think we'd also want to look back and think that each day with them had its purpose. Each day gave us strength. It taught us about the real meaning of love. We are better human beings because of them. Every single morning when we wake up and we're running around in the bedroom before we run down the hall to fire up the

Crowley Fun Machine for the day's activities, Aileen and I stop and listen down the hall. When we hear the whirr of Megan's machine and Patrick's machine, we smile, thank God, and then the whole craziness starts again. Another day. Thank God, another day.

The Diversity of Life

Trust means not just believing in family and God, but trusting in others as well. For the Crowley family, this has meant believing that our kids ought to experience as normal a life as possible—and trusting others to let them do so. It also shows how much they have to teach others.

When we moved to Princeton in 2002, we wanted Megan to go to the regular kindergarten that fall. New Jersey is very progressive about accommodating special needs, and the public schools are fantastic. That summer, we met with the counselors and a team came in to assess Megan and prepare an IEP, Individualized Education Program.

The school told us that they would try to accommodate Megan, but that she had extraordinary needs and they'd never had a kid like her in Princeton public schools. They had had a few autistic kids and a couple of children with cerebral palsy, but they had been in the habit of sending anybody profoundly affected to a county school. We looked at the county school, and it's a wonderful school doing wonderful things for some kids with very difficult situations. But it wasn't what Megan wanted. She wanted to be a regular kid among regular kids. For all that it ravages the muscles in people with Pompe, the disease never affects the mind. Megan, like Patrick and many other Pompe kids we have come to know, is amazingly smart and precocious. We wanted her in the public school.

So we went back and met with the principal, Dr. Ginsburg, and told him what we wanted, and he said, "Okay, we'll do it. We'll do our best to adjust. We'll make it work for Megan." And then he added, "But there's something I need you guys to do for me. Nobody in town really knows you both. You just moved here. I don't want there to be rumors or myths or anything. Let's just put it all out there. We have an orientation in August for the parents of all new incoming kindergartners where I speak and the teachers speak. Would you and Aileen come and speak to the parents about Megan?"

At first, I felt like, Why the heck should I have to explain my kid? But then I realized he was being very fair and it might help set the facts straight.

So Aileen and I went to the orientation at Johnson Park elementary school and I got up and talked to the fifty or so people in the room. We played a *Today* show tape that tells the story of Pompe disease and our family's efforts to develop a treatment. The program had originally aired in November 2001, and it followed Geeta Anand's first story about us, which had run in the *Wall Street Journal* in July. I didn't want the parents and teachers feeling sorry for Megan or us, just to show them this is who Megan is and this is our family. So after the tape, I explained, "We have a nurse, Sharon, who will go to school with Megan. Sharon is wonderful with kids, and Megs is an incredibly smart kid, despite her physical handicaps. She'll be careful with her wheelchair. She'll play great with all of your children."

The parents listened and generally appreciated what we discussed. I could sense, though, that some were uncomfortable, either with the subject or the awkwardness of our having to speak about Megan's special needs. So I injected a bit of humor. I continued by stating, "The doctors have told us there's very little chance of your children catching this Pompe... so long as Megan covers her nose when sneezing." It didn't exactly have the impact that I had hoped. Most people got it and kind of chuckled. But a couple of eyes lit up. Aileen shot me her patented stare, which connoted: "Knock off the wiseguy humor. Now." That went well.

Despite her father's mediocre presentation to her classmates' parents, Megan was allowed to enroll in kindergarten that fall. Megan got Lamont Fletcher for her teacher, a gentleman with decades of teaching experience. He treated Megan the same as all the other kids. Despite her physical limitations, he cut her no slack and cared for her no less than any of his other beloved students. She had an amazing year and made many friends.

I remember the day she got her first infusion of the enzyme therapy that saved her life in January of that kindergarten year. That afternoon, as she was getting her multi-hour infusion, her classmates called from the classroom to check on her. They each insisted on speaking with her directly. The call lasted nearly an hour.

In June 2003 Megan graduated kindergarten, another milestone. Dr. Ginsburg pulled me aside that afternoon and said, "John, I want to talk to you. We're looking forward to having Megan in first grade next year. She had a great year. She's an amazing kid."

I told him, "Thank you for everything you did, Bob. You and all the teachers were amazing, too. We could not have asked for more."

He told me, "I want to tell you something that you and Aileen need to know. After you gave that talk last summer, I had more than a handful of parents call, write, and e-mail me. Every one of them was the same story: 'The Crowleys seem like a lovely family, and we wish the best for their daughter. But my son/daughter is not used to this and this is an important first year. Please don't put my kid in little Megan's class.'"

My heart sank as the principal told me this. Megan had had a terrific year. She made great friends, many of whom are her closest confidantes to this day. She ran over only one kid's foot, and he was only out for a couple of days—not bad, I figured. On the first day of kindergarten, everybody was talking about themselves and their family and what they did during the summer. Mr. Fletcher did spend a little extra time with Megan that first day. He told the class, "This is Megan. She has a disease. Her voice sounds funny, and instead of walking she rides in this wheelchair. But like each of you, she's really smart." The kids got it immediately. From then on, Megan's classmates would explain her situation to others. If a substitute teacher or a new kid arrived, one of Megan's buddies would walk up, "This is my friend Megan. She's really cool. Her legs don't work and she can't breathe on her own, but her brain works great. She's just like us."

So it was distressing to think that even now, after a terrific year, parents might still be concerned. Had they not seen what we had seen these past nine months?

The principal continued, "The vast majority of parents were fine with it, but more than a handful were not, and I didn't pay them any attention. In fact, I actually made sure some of those kids were in Megan's class. The only reason I'm sharing this with you now is because in the last two weeks or so I've gotten calls, letters, and e-mails from most of the parents whose kids were in kindergarten with Megan. They all sent the same letter—"

I was thinking, "Here we go again. He's going to tell me they need Megan to go to a special school, after all. Too many parents are complaining."

He continued, "And their letters all said, 'Please, whatever you do, *please* put my kid in Megan's class next year. He/she learned so much from being in Megan's class and just adores her as well. She's one special little girl.'"

These fellow parents had learned about the special gifts that Megan had, not about her special needs.

They had indeed listened to and learned from their own children. It's remarkable what kids can teach us big people. Just as Megan and Patrick have taught Aileen and me so much about life and about ourselves, so too have they taught many others. We had placed our trust in our neighbors and their children. And they paid us back with loving-kindness and acceptance.

CHAPTER 2

NEVER, NEVER, NEVER QUIT

*Success is not final, failure is not fatal: it
is the courage to continue that counts.*
　　　　　　　—*Winston Churchill*

During the planning, writing, filming, and edit-
ing, the movie inspired by our family was called
The Untitled Crowley Project for so long that I began to
wonder if it was ever going to find its way onto theater marquees. There were other titles that were discussed—*So Defiant* and *Determined* were high among
the also-rans—and all reflected a core belief of our
family. In many respects, *Extraordinary Measures* captures it all perfectly: the grit, the uniqueness, the defiance, and, of course, the determination. It's not about
being the smartest or most talented or best connected.
It's about persistence and courage—and refusing to
quit in the face of an impossible challenge.

Having spent the first chapter discussing two
critical pillars of strength—trust and faith—I want to
spend some time on what might be the single most
important component of strength: determination.

Megan was diagnosed with Pompe disease on
March 13, 1998, exactly one week after Patrick was

born. He was with us in his infant car seat in the doctor's office when we got the news. Four months later, Patrick was also diagnosed with Pompe disease.

By autumn, Megan had rapidly deteriorated. She lost so much strength that when she got a simple cold, she developed pneumonia and lost the ability to breathe on her own. She ended up in the pediatric intensive care unit (PICU) of our local hospital in New Jersey. For hours, the doctors struggled to stabilize our twenty-month-old baby girl. We were told to expect the worst. Aileen and I prayed. "Please, God, if this be her fate, don't let her suffer anymore." If it had to come, we prayed, let it come quickly and peacefully.

After hours of agonized waiting, the head of the intensive care unit appeared. Aileen and I hugged, dreading to hear the words. Instead, he told us that Megan had stabilized and was breathing on a ventilator. The doctor was amazed. He told us we had some little fighter.

We entered the PICU and found Megan lying still and awake on the bed, tubes attached to what seemed like every vein in her little body. Her eyes darted around the room, inspecting all the action, and finally locked onto Aileen's eyes, as both of them burst into tears. Aileen and I knew that Megan didn't want to quit—and neither could we. I stroked my daughter's brown hair and told her, "Okay, Princess, if you want to fight, we'll fight, too."

That's the thing about strength and resolve. The more someone gives it, the more they have to give.

Megan's determination to survive Pompe disease only increased my determination to cure it.

We spent the next several years in a quest to help our children and all persons suffering from this little-understood, rare, and fatal disease. The search for an effective treatment was excruciating. Every time a breakthrough seemed around the corner, the research trail would hit a brick wall or the testing would yield a discouraging result. Two steps forward and one step back—and sometimes we even got that backward. And all the while, time marched on.

Megan and Patrick were growing weaker by the day, their enzymes unable to process the sugar stored as glycogen that fuels children with normally functioning cells. The unprocessed sugar not only deprives the cells of energy but also accumulates in the cells and leads to muscle atrophy so severe that patients eventually cannot eat or breathe without assistance. Other bodily systems are compromised as well. Germs that would lead to the sniffles in a healthy child present a deadly threat to someone whose body is weakened by this one defective gene on chromosome 17. Wheelchairs become a fact of life, as do ventilators and feeding tubes. If the disease cannot be controlled, then death arrives in the form of cardiac arrest or respiratory failure. For children diagnosed as young as Megan and Patrick were, death usually occurs in the first few years of life.

But if Megan could fight, then we could fight alongside her.

Over and over I've watched people and their families confront this deadly disease. In 1999, Baby John Koncel became the first child in the United States to receive an experimental enzyme replacement therapy treatment for Pompe disease. The enzyme had shown success in treating Japanese quail that had Pompe, actually strengthening some to the point where they regained flight. I spoke to John's parents, Deb and Barry Koncel, a few weeks before they made the decision to try the treatment on their little boy. I explained how frustrated I'd been by the maddening way a cure seemed to be a few months away but always fell through just as human trials were about to begin. They were from Chicago and I advised them, as a parent and as someone frantically growing knowledgeable about the field of Pompe research, that I wasn't sure it made sense to drag their very sick baby son all the way to North Carolina to the hospital at Duke Medical Center to enroll in a clinical study—and live for months on end in a hospital PICU. I actually saw Baby John right after the treatment began. He looked even weaker and more frail than Megan and Patrick, the totally limp "floppy baby" that typifies the most virulent form of infant-onset Pompe.

A month later I flew down to North Carolina to see for myself what had been described as a miracle by Y. T. Chen, a doctor not given to hyperbole. Aileen and I were accompanied on this trip by another doctor, Alfred Slonim, one of the world's leading Pompe experts, with whom we'd been exploring treatments for our kids. I couldn't believe my eyes when I saw Baby John. This beautiful little boy, who only a month earlier had lain there unable to move a muscle, sat on his mother's lap and cheerfully stretched his arms to play patty-cake. Even more promising was the echocardiogram that showed clear strengthening of Baby John's heart, the failure of which is the most common cause of death in Pompe victims.

I came back a couple of months later to visit the physician overseeing Baby John's treatment, and he told me Baby John wasn't doing very well. I visited him and saw a very sick, very weak little kid. He had begun to develop antibodies to the enzyme. Since Baby John was so small, the antibodies were particularly devastating and muted all the response to the enzymes he was receiving. The doctors tried many different ways to strengthen his immune system to tolerate the enzyme, but he just couldn't do it. Baby John eventually went home and his parents finally decided the enzyme wasn't working. It must have been brutal to watch their son, who had already been through so much, suffer as his body rebelled against the substance that represented his only chance at survival. They withdrew from the enzyme treatment and after a period of time Baby John died, at peace in his mother's arms at home in Chicago.

When we first began searching for a way to bring a treatment, any treatment, to Megan and Patrick, there were many who discouraged us. They weren't being callous. They were concerned about Aileen and me, and what the disappointment of a failed treatment would do to our already challenged family. We understood that.

Seeing Baby John initially benefit from this apparent miracle, I thought about the way I had hedged when his parents asked me about making the long trip from the Midwest for treatment. I thought about the look on his mother's face as her son sat up on her lap, smiling and laughing, under his own power for the first time. Aileen and I decided that for our family, we would stop at nothing to give our kids a shot at experiencing the sorts of memories that are taken for granted billions of times per day—extraordinary measures, indeed. I would never forget what it meant to other parents and other sick children to have not only those memories but the hope that those moments created.

It's impossible to know if those six months of hope and love that Baby John and his parents got while the treatment was effective were "worth it." A beautiful little boy spent a lot of time in a hospital far from home getting stuck with a lot of needles. I can't make that call for anyone else's family. But I saw the fight in Baby John just like I saw it in my kids, and I knew that I'd never stop fighting for those little moments.

Learn from Your Kids

One of the things Aileen and I have learned as parents of special needs children is how frequently we're the ones learning from them, rather than the other way around. We have learned more about life and love from our children than we have ever taught them. When it comes to perseverance, Megan in particular embodies the idea I'm thinking of when I say, "Never, never, never quit."

The emotional rollercoaster I describe with Baby John Koncel—the despair when no hope is in sight, the thrill when the child makes progress, and then the crushing disappointment when that progress evaporates—happened to Aileen and me with our kids. After years of struggle to develop a drug to treat Pompe and to get Megan and Patrick approved for that treatment, by the end of 2002, we finally secured spots for both of them in a clinical trial of a promising biotech drug. Adding even greater personal significance to the experiment was the fact that I had played a role in that drug's development. It is impossible to put into words what it felt like to see the medicine in those IV bags drip into my sick children, their bodies devastated by Pompe, their hearts twice the size they should have been. I remember joking to the nurse as he hooked up the tube, "Be careful with that treatment. It cost $200 million."

The first few months of 2003 were a magical time for our family. After Megan and Patrick began receiving their biweekly infusions, they responded almost immediately. Megan responded superbly, with her swollen heart and liver improving remarkably. Her progress had us envisioning a near future where she might be able to breathe without a ventilator, something unimaginable only months earlier. Patrick's heart, liver, and muscles responded positively as well, but not to the degree that Megan's did.

By the spring of that year, Megan was hanging out with me while I puttered around the house—the kind of mundane little joy that parents take for granted. I'd lift weights in the basement and she'd actually curl her little 2-pound dumbbells alongside me. It was both bonding time with Megs and physical therapy for her slowly strengthening muscles. The thrill Aileen and I got from just being able to watch TV with Megan sitting next to us on the couch made us appreciate the preciousness of every little moment.

My thirty-sixth birthday, April 7, 2003, was one such special day. Megs was a kindergartner and I got to go to school with her all day, and not just as her dad (though, thankfully, she had not yet reached the point of being embarrassed by this biological fact—that would, of course, come years later). Instead, I was her nurse that very snowy day. In early April a freak winter storm struck during midday. The response from school officials was typical: close the schools early, call the buses in, and send the children home as quickly as possible! Sending all those grade-schoolers onto buses that would try to maneuver on unplowed, not-yet-salted hilly roads was a stroke of administrative genius.

Back then, Megan had a "short bus" that could accommodate her wheelchair and would transport her to and from school. I have said many, many prayers of forgiveness for the jokes I laughed at during grammar school about the "short bus" kids. Aileen and I have cornered the market in Princeton on short buses. As the snowfall intensified, yellow short bus number

7 rolled up to the front of Johnson Park Elementary School in Princeton. Megan and her thirty-six-year-old former biotech executive–turned male nurse boarded the bus (or "snubnose," as we affectionately referred to it) and headed out down Rosedale Road for the four-mile trek home. We'd gone about two hundred yards when short bus number 7 slid off the road and into a slight embankment. It was a slow slide and we were fine. Megan's wheelchair was strapped in tightly, and with her newfound strength she held her head and arms securely in the chair. But we were stuck, way stuck. I called Aileen and she rushed out in her SUV to help.

We transferred Megan out of her wheelchair. The chair would be spending the evening inside short bus number 7, but thankfully we would not. Aileen had Patrick and all his medical equipment latched into a car seat. John Jr. sat next to him to make sure neither Patrick nor his life support equipment slid across the car. Aileen had no time to find Megan's car seat. It was buried in the basement and had not been used in years. We had planned to improvise and just lay her securely across the backseat while I held her in place for the short but perilous ride home, but Megan insisted that she sit upright and be secured by a seatbelt. She had never in her life ridden in a car in anything other than a wheelchair or a car seat. But we tried it. She looked secure. Nonetheless, I sat closely next to her and wrapped my arm tightly around her. We began to move. Megan insisted that she did not need help (i.e., in her highly precocious way: "Let go of me, you overprotective zealot"). And so I did. And she sat still, as firmly in control of her upper body as her mom was of the three-ton SUV. We made it home safely. Megan was getting stronger. It had been eighty-eight days since she had received her first enzyme infusion. That is still the best birthday gift I've ever received.

But success can be fleeting.

About two months later, I was busy in some intense business travels, including for the first time evaluating the technology of business opportunities at Amicus, the biotech company where I would eventually work. After a few weeks of neglecting our mutual workout routines, I corralled Megan and brought her down to the basement for a little daddy-daughter time and a workout. Megan grabbed the 2-pound dumbbells she'd managed easily a few weeks earlier and struggled to lift them. "C'mon, Megs," I urged. "You're just rusty from taking a couple weeks off from our routine. Work it. Remember, pain is weakness leaving the body."*

Lack of effort wasn't what was holding Megan back, however. The progress she and Patrick had been making from the treatment had slowed and the remarkable increases in skeletal muscle strength had begun

---

*Megan has never been a fan of my military motivational clichés, but I figured I'd at least try. She did always get a kick out of, "Remember what second place is…first loser." In this instance, at least, I was savvy enough not to hit her with: "That which doesn't kill us only makes us stronger." I figured of everyone I know, Megan least needed reminding of that.

to wear off to a degree. It was heartbreaking for the kids and devastating for Aileen and me when we fully grasped that the upward trajectory of improvement in strength was in fact waning. We had dared to envision a more normal future for our children, dared to whisper of an almost normal life for them. But those whispers became ever more faint against the reality of the relentless progression of this horrible disease.

The realization that Megan and Patrick were not going to be totally cured was a setback, yes. Knowing full well then that they were unlikely ever to lead "normal" lives was a blow after so many years of hard work and hope, especially after having glimpsed a tiny bit of what better health would be like for them and for our whole family. But we began to realize what we had accomplished for our kids. This enzyme therapy treatment had extended their lives, likely for many years (if not decades). It fixed their hearts, which had been twice the normal size. On echocardiogram, today you still cannot tell their hearts from those of a healthy child. We extended and enhanced the quality of their lives. It is virtually certain that they'd have been dead without the enzyme, which they continue to receive every other week. Moreover, as the treatment has advanced—the infusions now last six hours instead of four and are given to kids at an earlier diagnosis point than was available to Megan and Patrick—it has had even more profound effects. Science progresses, we all learned, and we all came to more fully appreciate each day, each step forward, and each incremental improvement in life.

Who could ever assign a value to what those several months of stronger living were worth to the kids and to our family? I thought about Megan's defiant eyes from five years earlier, when she refused to die in the pediatric intensive care unit. It is clear to Aileen and me that the best measure of a life is not the quantity of the years in which it's lived, but the quality of those years.

Examples of my kids inspiring me to refuse to quit are not only rooted in life-or-death matters. Sometimes it's just seeing the way they overcome enormous challenges simply to get through the day. It's difficult to see a nine-year-old gasp for breath as a ventilator alarm signals a blockage that must be removed from his throat—a near daily occurrence—and not get a sense of perspective about the silly little things in life that may be bugging you.

At the peak of their popularity, the Jonas Brothers included a stop in Philadelphia on their summer 2009 tour. Megan informed us that she'd be in attendance, no matter what. (I'm pretty sure she thinks that my assistant, Jeanette, and I actually work for Ticketmaster.) And so I bought eight tickets so Aileen could take Megan and six of Megan's friends to the concert.

Unfortunately, a couple of days before the event, Megan came down with flu-like symptoms. That should be enough for any parent to order that the concert be skipped, but especially in the case of a twelve-year-old girl on a ventilator with a severely compromised respiratory system. Megan wouldn't hear of it. Even when her fever hit 101.5 degrees, she was adamant. I called her that afternoon and started to say, "Megs, honey..." She recognized the letting-her-down-easy tone and immediately replied, "No, I feel fine. I'm definitely going." I thought about all the things Megan had not been able to participate in throughout her short lifetime. Not just running and jumping every single day, but the endless doctor appointments and treatment sessions that yanked her from her friends and her routines and her schoolwork, in which she took enormous pride and satisfaction.

I said, "You know what? It's fine. Go to the concert."

Megan replied, "Yeah, well, it's not fine according to mom. She's giving me trouble. You better talk to her because there's no way I'm staying home. *You* straighten her out." (Megan remains under the impression that I have the ability to sway her equally obstinate mother....I allow the illusion to persist. Dignity is important.)

Aileen loaded up the handicapped-accessible minivan. Of course it was pouring rain, "Crowley luck" being an Irish cousin of Murphy's Law, as she headed off to Philly in rush-hour traffic.

With handicapped seats at large venues, you either get the best seats in the house or the worst. At the Wachovia Center it happens to be the latter, so the whole gang headed for the upper deck, chirping with delight at the thought of being in the same zip code as the three adorable (and actually quite well-grounded) mop-topped brothers.

Directly in front of the gang were two rather large middle-aged women in tank tops who stood in the sight lines of the handicapped section the entire time. The Jonas Brothers (or "Joe-Bros," as their adoring young fans refer to them) attract all sorts, but the great majority of their fans are the teen and preteen crowd. These two fans in front of Megs were a tad out of place. They ate copious amounts of the remarkably unhealthy stadium cuisine, and every time they finished an item, they'd place the empty box or wrapper on the floor of the handicapped section. They knew every word to every song, and Aileen and the girls tried to catch a glimpse of the Jonas Brothers through the wall of women in front of them.

None of that mattered to Megan. She was in her element, thrilled to be at the concert and grateful that we had gotten tickets for her friends. But she was still feeling pretty crummy, and when Aileen looked over, she noticed Megan sniffling. She said, "Oh, Meg, your nose is running."

Megan replied, expressing her ever sharp wit, "Yeah, I'm surprised it's not blood because of these lousy seats Daddy got us." Clearly, her Ticketmaster broker in the bedroom down the hall had failed to live up to expectations.

Megan's determination to attend that concert exemplifies the spirit of never, never quitting. My little girl has spent a great deal of her life in hospitals. She spends every minute of her life with tubes in her throat and every waking hour in a wheelchair or lying in bed. The simple act of taking a shower is an hour-long chore with much-needed help from her nurses. Megs has never been out of eyesight or earshot of an adult in her entire life. Nonetheless, her determination to enjoy these special opportunities—and believe me, for a twelve-year-old girl there is nothing more special than the Jonas Brothers—represents not just a chance to create an amazing memory. It shows a spirit of defiance, a refusal to allow challenges and disappointments to extinguish her zest for life. To Megan, this is who she is, and it's the rest of the world that has to adjust—or just treat her like everyone else. No better, no worse. We are all special in different ways.

Patrick is a much quieter kid. He isn't nearly as extroverted as Megan and dislikes crowds and loud, noisy places. But he has a sweetness to him, a gentleness, that is heartbreakingly lovable. Underlying that sweet persona is a different but equally intense sense of determination.

Patrick is not quite as vigorous as Megan. He's unable to muster the strength and coordination to operate the joystick on an electric wheelchair, so he's far more dependent on his nurses and Aileen and me for mobility. He also cannot speak as forcefully. But whereas Megan never gets frustrated by the difficulty many people have in understanding her words through the ventilator, Patrick is shyer about his voice and less forceful in asserting it.

When Patrick was born, he was bigger and stronger than Megan and even John had been. We were living in California at the time, ecstatic over the arrival of our third child. Patrick was Aileen's third C-section. We were friendly with the doctor, and I remember him handing over our 10-pound son and saying, "Whoa, we've got a moose here." He sized up my 5'6" frame and joked, "His real dad must be a big man." I said, "Thanks," and Aileen smilingly chided us to knock it off.

Megan's diagnosis hit when Patrick was a week old. We knew enough about simple genetics to understand that there was a 25 percent chance Patrick would also have Pompe disease. But for the first couple of months of Patrick's life, we just couldn't believe that was possible; he was so strong.

Looking back at Megan's first few weeks, there were signs that all was not right: she wasn't holding her head up at eight weeks, and her tongue was bigger than it should have been. We didn't dwell on it. But when we look back today at her baby pictures, knowing what we know now, we can see the early signs.

With Patrick there was none of that. He was bouncing in his Jolly jumper, strong and happy as any baby. We're all complex individuals. Megan and Patrick have the same genetic mutation that causes Pompe disease, but they also have 50,000 or so other genes. As an infant, Patrick was stronger than Megan had been. But from about his first birthday, somehow Patrick's genes didn't compensate as well as Megan's did, and by the time he was about three years old, he was on a very different slope than Megan. That more intense battle with the devastating effects of Pompe has certainly helped to shape some of his experiences, but even when he was little, we used to call him our gentle little giant. He was just naturally so sweet and reserved, whereas Megan had a much more assertive personality and would usually end up getting her own way.

Because Pompe disease attacks the muscles, someone with an advanced form retains the ability to move only the parts of the body that can be controlled by tendons alone. By the time he was six years old, Patrick was really struggling with gross motor strength, and by eight years old, his fine motor skills were largely gone, to the point where he could barely move his body at all. Wiggling his fingers and toes, moving his eyes, and making small facial expressions (sticking out his tongue is his favorite act of defiance) are about it. Think of the famed physicist and author Stephen Hawking, but as a young boy. Patrick's physical condition and gentle personality combine to make it all the more touching when he does assert himself.

He had seen his brother and his cousins taking karate and one day he announced to Aileen, "I want to take karate." She found a local karate studio that held a Saturday afternoon session for kids with special needs—one kid had Down syndrome, another was autistic, another had cerebral palsy. For over a year now, I've been taking Patrick and moving his arms and legs around. He loves the time with me and it really does help his self-confidence.

One summer, I had John and Patrick out by the pool, and I said, "Come on, guys, we're going to do some work in the pool." I told John to take the skimmer and get the leaves out of the pool. As he was doing it, he started in a little bit on Patrick.

"Patrick, see how strong I am? I can do this man's work. Ha-ha, you can't do it because you're a wimp." Patrick narrowed his brow and his eyes got intense. He took a deep breath and he put his chest out as much as could and he said, clear as day, "Hey, I ain't no wimp. Get over here. I'll kick your ass!"

John stopped skimming and yelled, "Dad, Patrick said a bad word."

I dutifully reprimanded him for swearing while secretly swelling up with pride that my son had stood up for himself, that a kid who couldn't move a muscle had said, "Get over here. I'll kick your ass." It was eerily reminiscent of the scene in *Monty Python and the Holy Grail* when the brave knight lost arms and legs and mightily stood his ground and insisted that his opponent stand and fight: "It's just a flesh wound." Mind over matter, strength of character, and pride in self. Patrick, with his defiant, mildly inappropriate comment, had stood for it all. And then some. You go, little man, you go. And, for the record, his big brother never called him a wimp again.

No Pity Parties, Please

Another way my kids have taught me perseverance is in refusing to feel sorry for themselves. It's easy to throw a big pity party after every setback in life. Kids with far less serious challenges than Megan and Patrick would be forgiven for thinking, "God, this sucks and I wish we had this and I wish that were different." It's fine to think about those things and act to change the things you can. But idly feeling sorry for yourself accomplishes nothing.

One evening in October 2005, I was putting Megan to bed and we were saying our prayers. She had heard mention that day of a bad earthquake in Pakistan, in which hundreds of kids had been killed.

"Daddy," she said. "I saw an earthquake on the news. Did you see it?"

"Yeah, I did honey," I told her. "It's just awful."

"We've got to pray for those kids," she said.

I looked at her with an overflowing heart. I never think of Megan as "different," but she is, and watched this little kid who can't get out of bed, can't take care of herself, hooked up to a ventilator with her hands in front of her, deeply in prayer for kids from a part of the world she had never heard of until a few hours earlier.

I thought about all the times that we had prayed together—for kids we didn't know, for Grandpa John in heaven, for a sick family member. It dawned on me then: Never once in all these quiet moments of prayer had Megan ever uttered, "Can we say a prayer for me?" or "Can we pray that my medicine works better? or that God makes me stronger or makes me live longer?" or even "Can I do better on my test tomorrow?" I can't remember a single time she ever expressed a trace of self-pity or even the slightest hint that she wished things were different for herself. No one ever sat Megan down and delineated things that are appropriate in prayers. It's just not in her nature to ask for herself. Honestly, if there's anyone Megan pities, it's everybody else because they're not as smart or dynamic as she is, poor things.

Megan's outlook on life has inspired Aileen and me every step of the way. She is the most remarkable little lady and has touched and inspired everyone she has ever met. And I mean everyone.

Megan is getting to the age where girls become interested in boys. It's the age, too, where young girls dream of their lives as adult women. One day we were talking about growing up and getting married and having kids, and Megan wheeled closer to me. She said: "Can you keep a secret?" I replied, in proud reference to my years as a naval intelligence officer, "Megs, I am *very* good at keeping secrets. Especially yours." She nodded and asked me to follow her to the guest bedroom across the hall. She instructed me to open the closet, and I dutifully complied. She then pointed to the bottom drawer in the closet and told me to open it. Hidden under a stack of old clothes was a giant spiral notebook that she had clearly been working on for months. The book contained elaborate plans for her wedding: the music, her bridesmaids and their dresses, her invitations, flowers, registry, groomsmen's gifts—everything. When I read on her song list a line that stated: "Song for me and Daddy to dance to: 'The Way You Look Tonight,'" I about lost it. The strength she showed when she refused to die at twenty months is precisely the same spirit that has her envisioning a future that includes a fairy-tale wedding.

It's been said that courage is strength under adversity. Every day of Megs' life is marked by an adversity that most of us could not even imagine. And yet she handles it with grace and confidence. It is that gift, that ability to transcend what "should" be and make it into what you want it to be that makes her such a gift from God. You go, girl. And, again for the record, she "cleared" me to share the wedding planning story here, otherwise I would have held the secret!

When Megan was little I used to tell her, "You know, Megs, we're making special medicine and someday you'll get out of that wheelchair and you'll walk." And then it was, "You know what, Megan, maybe you're not going to walk, but you're going to breathe without your tubes." And for that period of time when she first started on the enzyme, those first six or nine months, she really was getting much stronger. We were developing protocols and I was flying around the country to see doctors and exploring the very real possibility of Pompe kids strengthening to the point where they could breathe without the ventilator. And then she started to slowly regress.

Now we don't talk like that. We don't say, "Megan, you're going to walk," "Megan, you're going to get off your breathing machine." Instead, we talk about life experiences. "Megan, you're going to be a seventh grader next year." And Megan carries forth with her plans. Not just her wedding. She is thinking about her prom and planning her Sweet 16 and is positive that she will drive one day. And who the heck knows? We have learned to take one day at a time. And we don't hope for miracles. We make them.

Meanwhile, we try to balance our hopes and optimism with a degree of reality and an ever-present good sense of humor. We are a family of wiseasses (that's the Irish in us). Shortly after I found that book of wedding plans, Megan and I were at the movies together. During the film, I had to suction her and spit was flying all over the movie theater and she was even throwing up a little bit. I said, "Megs, you're just going to be a dream date someday." She replied, "Oh, I know, just beautiful. Sooooo romantic."

After report cards came at the end of the school year in 2009, I got home late from work and Megan came whizzing by in her wheelchair to show me her marks. She got straight As, as usual. But she had also managed to stop by John Jr.'s room on her way to show me her triumph. She wanted me to see his report card as well, to point out that he'd received all Bs—which is very good for him, and I know he worked hard to achieve it.

I don't know a single adult who maintains that level of perspective. Myself included. Anytime I think, "Oh God, work just sucks, this or that is so unfair, I'm done with this, I'm tired"—whatever the complaint or moan of the day may be, I try to catch myself. "Enough. Think of everything you've got and live each day like it was your last and stop feeling sorry for yourself. That's too easy. And life is too good. One day at a time. So by the grace of God, pray for another."

CHAPTER 3

YOU CAN'T DO IT ALONE

You've strung together a few successes. Accomplished a few impressive goals. Just as you're starting to feel pretty good about yourself ... that's when it's most critical to open your heart and let others help.

Asking others for help remains very difficult for me. Even allowing others to help does not come naturally. Losing my father at a young age drilled into me the importance of self-reliance. I have based my life on the principle of not accepting "It cannot be done," so it's not always easy to admit that I have to rely on others. But I have come to learn that there are times when asking for assistance is necessary. Beyond that, sometimes the act of receiving assistance not only solves the problem at hand, but uplifts both me and those doing the helping, and bonds us more tightly.

By the time I started law school at Notre Dame in September 1989, Aileen and I were feeling pretty good about where our lives seemed to be headed. For an Irish cop's kid, South Bend, Indiana, was in many ways sacred ground. I thought back to the New Year's Day in 1975 when my dad and I saw the Fighting Irish edge

Alabama in what was the very first and the very last Notre Dame game we ever saw together. Now, some fifteen years later, I had arrived in South Bend as a young man ready to take on the legal world.

Aileen was excited as well. Having moved all over the country as a "GE brat," she didn't identify any particular place as her hometown. Having spent some of her teens in neighboring Kentucky, and with her parents just a few hours south in Indianapolis, this felt as much like home to her as anywhere.

It was a great time for us. We married in 1990 between my first and second year of law school. We had a fairy-tale wedding and then got our first apartment together, in the fabulous metropolis of Mishawaka, Indiana, not far from Notre Dame's campus. We'd go to all the football games together, and her high school friends would visit. It was wonderful to be young and in love and have our whole lives in front of us. Our rent was $300 a month. Life was sweet at the Candlewood Apartments off Grape Road.

Aileen got a job as the assistant manager of the Ralph Lauren Polo Outlet in Michigan City, Indiana. She would commute an hour each way and work very long hours to earn $16,500 a year. But my usual obsession with achieving top grades—combined with a heavy outside workload as a law clerk, since I was paying much of my own tuition—meant that we didn't see each other all that much.

That only intensified after my second year of law school, when I took a summer internship with the prestigious Indianapolis law firm of Bingham Summers Welsh & Spilman. At $1,000 a week, I was going to make almost as much in a summer as we had been making in a year.

Bingham Summers treated their summer associates to adventures like the Indianapolis 500 and the Colts camp. It was a great place, and I remain close to many of my colleagues there to this day. I decided to accept the firm's offer to continue working there part-time during my third year of law school: twenty hours a week at $20 an hour.

With me working in Indianapolis, near where her parents lived, Aileen decided to move into her parents' house, and I'd stay with them while I was in Indianapolis. These days, having to move is just about my biggest fear, but back then, it was nothing to pack up a U-Haul and relocate every six months. It was a terrific time for us. Aileen's father had been promoted to president of the RCA division and was actually involved in renaming the Hoosier Dome the RCA Dome. He'd done pretty well for a kid from Scranton. They had an enormous home, and we stayed in one of their bedrooms to save some money. We had decided to buy a home, and this gave us an opportunity to pull together a small down payment.

Eventually, we got a tiny apartment in Indianapolis, and I worked my schedule so I had classes only on Tuesdays and Thursdays. I would start the drive up to South Bend at 4:00 a.m. on Tuesday and stay for eighteen hours of classes and study groups, then drive back to Indianapolis. I worked at Bingham Summers on Mondays, Wednesdays, and Fridays. Back then, Indiana law students could take the bar exam before graduating law school, so I was also studying for the bar, which I took in February of my third year, while continuing to work those twenty hours and going to law school as a long-distance commuter. I worked like a madman, and we saved every penny we could.

We liked Indianapolis so much that we started to consider making it our permanent home. By early in my third year of law school, I had an offer in hand from Bingham Summers at a starting salary of $55,000, which went very far in Indiana back then. I also had interviewed with some firms in Chicago and New York, and had offers from them as well for somewhat more money. By then, however, we had bought our first home: $179,000 for a brand-new house just north of Indianapolis. I remember the pride I felt in having saved the down payment ourselves, about $20,000, from work and wedding gifts.

Aileen, meanwhile, had left the Polo outlet job when we moved to Indianapolis, and gotten a job in a department store in Indianapolis. With her growing experience in retail and fresh off being a new bride, we decided to buy a tiny bridal shop. Aileen ran the daily operations and managed the store, while I helped with the blocking and tackling of running a business, handling most of the hiring, buying inventory, and managing cash flow (or lack thereof). Aileen grew the business beautifully, eventually opening a second store.

As anyone who's ever started a retail business knows, it's no picnic. There is no vacation. There is no time away. It is your life. When husband and wife are in it together, there's no such thing as leaving your work at the office; it's on your minds constantly. We'd be near panic about meeting an upcoming payroll and we'd borrow to keep the lights on, and just when it'd look as though we weren't going to make it, sales would explode and we'd think, "Great! We're going to be rich!"

Until we realized that cash flow management was just as important as sales, because we still couldn't make payroll after we'd used all that incoming revenue to buy inventory. Looking back, I believe that if I knew then what I know now, it could have been a pretty successful business. As it was, it's a minor miracle that we managed to stay afloat for three-plus years, and sell well over 1,000 wedding gowns in the process. Meanwhile, my own lifelong interest in business had grown into a passion. I decided to pursue an MBA. I was accepted at the only school I applied to, the Harvard Business School. Aileen, always a trouper and willing to support me in my evolving school and career decisions, was up for the move to Boston. As we did with much of our life, we viewed it as an adventure. But by then the bridal shop was starting to struggle, anyway, and Aileen's parents had moved once again, this time back to New Jersey. There was no way she could be expected to stay in Indianapolis alone, amid the shop's struggles, especially since we had just been blessed by the arrival of our first child, John Francis Crowley III (John Jr. for short), born on December 21, 1994.

I wouldn't begin at the Harvard Business School until January 1996, so our plan was for Aileen and the baby to join her parents in New Jersey in September, while I stayed in Indianapolis and wrapped up some cases at the law firm. We tried to save what we could while also trying to sell the house and wind down the business.

Unfortunately, winding down the business was easier said than done. Having practiced law during those years of getting the shop off the ground, I had managed to save maybe $10,000, and I had another $20,000 or so in my 401(k) at the firm. Every penny of that had to go toward the loans we had taken on the business and early-termination penalties on the shop's leases. And, of course, I had plenty of law school debt as well. To put it in complex personal financial terms: We were screwed.

We faced the first real financial jam of our marriage. I had personally guaranteed these loans and leases—another business lesson learned the hard way. But at the time, we'd look at a beautiful retail location and say, "Wow, we can rent this whole big store, and all I have to do is sign this piece of paper?" My credit history, then and now, has always been pristine and, as a lawyer on his way to one of the world's most prestigious (and expensive) business schools, I couldn't risk having my credit destroyed.

We knew we'd be selling our house, but with so little time to build equity, we'd be lucky to get enough to pay the commission and cover our mortgage balance. Further, I'd need to borrow even more money to pay my business school tuition. I knew that we had no choice. I would have to talk to Aileen's father.

Marty Holleran is someone I respect as much as anyone I've ever known. I suppose in some sense I was always looking for mentorship from a father figure. In Marty, I had someone who was not only father to the wonderful woman I intended to spend my life with, but was also a thoughtful and learned man of the world, a guy who had worked his way to the pinnacle of corporate America from the most humble of backgrounds but remained a warm and loving and decent man.

Marty has always had my respect, as he earned every penny he ever had, having grown up poor in Scranton, Pennsylvania. He expected the same from me. Although he was very generous with us—throwing a lavish wedding at his home and giving us $5,000 for a wedding gift—he expected me to support his daughter without handouts from him or anyone else. He never made anyone feel inferior for not having the material success he has had.

That's not to say he wasn't proud of what he'd achieved. But there's a meaningful difference between flaunting what you have and being proud to have provided for your family. He didn't buy a big house so he could tell people he lived in a big house. He bought a big house because it was a wonderful place for his kids to grow up, and because he had a way of making his home the center of his children's lives for social events and parties. It made life better and more enjoyable for his family. When he moved to Indianapolis, he did the same thing.

Asking Marty for help was one of the most difficult things I've ever had to do. I put it off, hoping for some kind of miracle, until lawyers for the leasing agent began to call to tell me I owed all this money. When I went to visit Aileen and John Jr. at her parents' new home in New Jersey for the weekend, I shored up my courage and approached Marty. I prepared spreadsheets and charts, and explained to him that I'd be able to take care of every detail except this one lease obligation and a bank line of credit. In all, we owed about $100,000 to wind down the affairs of the bridal shop. Now, Marty was a very successful guy, but not wealthy. He didn't have that kind of cash just lying around; he'd have to draw down a home equity loan to come up with it.

And so it was done. Marty gave me the money, no questions asked. Naturally, I couldn't repay him during business school. Quite frankly, I wasn't sure how I would ever be able to come up with that sum of money—not in his lifetime, I thought (and maybe not even in mine). With Megan and then Patrick arriving right afterward, along with all the attendant expenses their care and the search for a cure would entail, I couldn't make a single payment then, either. And yet, Marty never said a word about it.

Nearly six years later, I was poised to sell the bio-tech company that I had started to find a cure for our children's Pompe disease. Even amid all the talk of a big number for the acquisition, Marty never mentioned the loan. When we sold the company in 2001, my share came to about $6 million. The first check I wrote was to pay off all my student loans, $142,000 worth. The second check I wrote was to Aileen's dad for $100,000. He was visiting and I just gave him an envelope and said simply, "Thanks." Neither of us has ever mentioned it again.

This is what I mean by "you can't do it alone." I tried as hard as I could to avoid asking Marty for help. But in the end, I'm glad that circumstances made it impossible not to seek his assistance. My father-in-law rescuing us like that was not only a financial lifeline at a time when we really needed it, but more important, it established a bond between the two of us stronger than we ever could have had otherwise. I knew my father-in-law was the kind of man who would help me out in a jam, no questions asked. And he knew that I was the kind of man who would honor my commitments without being reminded. And it set an example of how we in time would respond to help family and friends as we developed the means to assist.

That's exactly what happened a few months after we first heard the words "Pompe disease" in March

1998, when we were living in northern California, after I had completed business school in June 1997.

We knew virtually nothing about it and had a very difficult time finding anyone who could tell us more. As with a lot of rare diseases—especially in the era before the Internet became the world's knowledge repository—those confronting Pompe disease could not easily find doctors who specialized in it or even other families to share information and look to for support.

When I started looking for answers right after Megan's diagnosis, I found a couple of scientists in the United States and a team of researchers in Europe. I contacted them all and began asking as many questions as they'd endure about Pompe and enzyme replacement therapies and other lysosomal storage disorders like Gaucher and Tay-Sachs. Each doctor and scientist mentioned feeling that progress could be made if only there were money to conduct clinical trials. To raise that money and move the science forward, Aileen and I founded a charity and began raising money.

I had never started a charity before. Quite frankly, until the kids' diagnosis, I had never given much thought to charitable causes. Sure, I'd give when someone specifically asked, but that was limited to a few specific causes, like our local church, and in very limited amounts. Charitable giving just wasn't something that was part of a struggling young couple's life. Like a lot of thirty-year-old type-A guys, I had been entirely focused on building my career and providing for my family. Now, I'd have to learn how to start a foundation, and I'd need to rely on others to help fund it.

Harvard Business School provides not only an invaluable source of future business contacts, but also puts you through a rigorous shared experience with people who go on to the highest echelons of business. Our family names weren't exactly associated with the pillars of wealth and high society. Lots of awesome people in my family, and no shortage of cops, for sure, but "trust fund babies" were nowhere to be found on the Crowley or Valentino family trees (and, believe me, I looked). So my HBS classmates, many of whom had come from similarly humble backgrounds on their way to great success, were the natural place for me to start raising funds for the foundation.

Nearly every one of my classmates kicked in something—sometimes a check for $500 or a pledge to raise $1000, but most often modest amounts. Within a month or two, we had raised over $50,000. Within the small world of Pompe disease, that was a huge amount. I remember sitting at my in-laws' kitchen table with Aileen's father and looking at our Christmas card list and writing a personal letter to as many of those people as we could. We were building a fundraising network one person at a time. Feeling helpless about the kids' diagnosis, we felt incredibly inspired to receive this enormous outpouring of support, to realize that we weren't alone in this fight to find a cure.

In December 1998, I attended a research conference devoted to Pompe at the National Institutes of

Health. It was there that we saw the presentation of the Enzyme Replacement Therapy that formed the basis of my first company, Novazyme. Less than three years later, that company was acquired by Genzyme, the world's third-largest biotech company, in a nine-figure deal.

None of that could have occurred without the willingness of my business school classmates to pick up the phone looking for a few bucks to cure a disease virtually no one had even heard of. As with the loan from Aileen's father, it wasn't only the recipients of this kindness—myself, my kids, and really all people with Pompe disease—who benefited. The ones who donated their time and money benefited as well. Time and again, my classmates have told me how much it meant to them to be a part of something meaningful, in the face of such incredible odds. Many of them had taken high-pressure jobs at firms where new hires had to prove themselves with marathon hours in robotic corporate environments. They viewed the opportunity as a favor to them, rather than the other way around. Once again, the circular grace of reaching out to others had made itself clear.

After these experiences, Aileen and I vowed that we would do our best to support the causes of those near to us, to the best of our ability. If someone needed help and was lucky enough to know someone who knew us, and if I was lucky enough to have the resources to help, then we'd help. Aileen and I have since given away about 20 percent of everything we've ever made.

And we are grateful for the opportunity to give. Giving to multiple charitable causes has helped us at least as much as it's helped the recipient. It is part of what makes America great.

After Megan and Patrick were diagnosed with Pompe disease, a solitary goal began to crystallize in my imagination: save my kids. Save their lives, extend their lives, improve their lives, not just for my own family but for all families affected by Pompe disease. My job in San Francisco as a management consultant working on banking mergers was not the ideal platform to advance that goal. After the kids' diagnosis, I had taken serious steps to educate myself about Pompe and push the science forward, but I wanted to be personally involved on a daily basis. I also wanted the kids to be nearer the best treatments, many of which were in and around my home state, New Jersey, "America's pharmacy."

Aileen and I were also beginning to get our arms around the challenges our family would face financially, logistically, and emotionally. Two kids in wheelchairs and on ventilators with a disease would require twenty-four-hour care from nurses experienced in things like clearing a clogged trachea. And parents of kids with extraordinary medical concerns need to learn to care for the kids as well as any nurse or respiratory therapist. To help deal with these challenges, I took a job in central New Jersey in the summer of 1998 with Bristol-Myers Squibb ("BMS"), one of the world's largest pharmaceutical companies, where I would work for almost two years. The ability to be involved with health care on a daily basis, to work for a great company whose mission statement was, literally, "to extend and enhance human life," the proximity of treatments and family, and the outstanding benefits, especially health care, made it an easy decision.

My colleagues were supportive of my personal efforts to work on Pompe, even though that was outside the scope of my official duties at Bristol-Myers Squibb. But the real support came when I was asked to become the CEO of the embryonic company that I'd helped found. The reaction to this radical career change from my bosses at BMS was instantaneous: "Go. If you find the cure and your kids get better, then a lot of others will also benefit and you'll make as much money as you need to take care of your family. If you don't find the cure, then you will always have a place here." That support helped me go forward and create the drug now taken by a thousand people with Pompe disease. To succeed in this venture required a capacity for risk taking, the mark of every entrepreneur. Without the desire to help drive science toward a treatment for Pompe as the motivation for starting a business, I doubt that I would have had the cojones to take this great risk. But I did.

Friends Helping Friends

My best friend for nearly twenty-five years now is Ed Devinney. I know him as Ed. My kids know him as "Uncle Ed." Most people, though, refer to him as

Commander Edward Devinney, United States Navy. His shipmates today simply call him Captain; he is the current commanding officer of the pride of the Navy, the U.S.S. *Cole*. The Cole was the warship attacked by Al-Qaeda terrorists in the Mideast in 2000, killing seventeen American sailors.

I've known Ed since the days when we both held much less lofty positions. We were roommates during my first year at the Naval Academy in 1986. When Aileen and I were struggling with our marriage, Ed was a great listener. He had known tough times in life in other circumstances, so he didn't cross-examine me about it. He never told me to quit whining and shut the hell up. And I whined a bunch back then. But at the right times he'd ask the big questions: "Is this a decision you really want to make tonight?" or "What do you envision for yourself five or ten years from now? And for Aileen? And the kids?"

At the time I was relying on Ed for the counseling that only a best friend can provide, he too was experiencing tough times. Ed's mother had struggled with breast cancer for more than a decade. She had actually been diagnosed back when we were midshipmen at Annapolis. Now, his mother's health had taken a bad turn. Her cancer had returned and had metastasized. Nearly every weekend, Ed would trek from Washington to Doylestown, Pennsylvania, to spend time with his mom. I went with Ed a number of times to visit her in hospice as the end drew near. Mrs. Devinney had been a wonderful lady, dignified and serene. Even as her health deteriorated, she was always concerned with my family and would always ask how she could help. Every time I would enter her room, her first words would always be: "How are the kids?"

On January 12, 2000, Ed called me at 7:00 a.m. to let us know she had passed away an hour and a half or so earlier and that he had been by her side. That placed her date and time of death precisely twenty-five years after that of my dad's. We reflected on the remarkable coincidence. He even mentioned that he hoped my dad would be there among so many others to welcome her to heaven. We then talked briefly about funeral plans. Suddenly, Ed remembered he had just been promoted in the Navy from Lieutenant to Lieutenant Commander. He had his Lieutenant uniform with him in Pennsylvania, not his dress blues Lieutenant Commander uniform. Ed's mom never got to see him wear the Lieutenant Commander's rank. She was so very proud of her son's service, as well she should have been.

"What am I going to do?" he pleaded. "I don't have the right uniform!" He really wanted to say goodbye to her with the proper rank. I simply told Ed, "Don't worry, you'll have it by this evening." And without hesitation, Aileen and I jumped in the car and made the five-hour drive to Virginia to get Ed's uniform and bring it back.

Ed's mother was buried on January 15, the same day my dad had been buried. Ed was very loving but very stoic throughout—until the graveside. It was bitterly cold and everyone left a rose or a card on the casket and made their way out of the cemetery. Ed couldn't bring himself to leave. He started to get emotional, and I put my hand on his shoulder.

"Crowls, I don't want to go," he said. "I don't want to leave her."

We stood there for a while longer, then I said, "Ed, it's time to go."

"No, I don't want to leave her," he said again.

"Ed, she's not here," I told him gently. "I can't promise you there's a heaven, but if there is, she's there. And if not, she's with you and your dad and sister, always."

Maybe it was a platitude. But when people are hurting, what they need is not the perfectly uttered magic phrase. A hand on a shoulder and some simple words of solace are all it takes, just knowing that you are not alone. It is that most human of connections and bonds that hold us together in the toughest and darkest moments. You cannot do it alone. To this day, we still always touch base every January 12.

Finally, we've also learned that allowing others to help doesn't only help us. Sometimes, it helps them as well.

The Kindness of Strangers

In 2004, we went to New York City for a three-day weekend to celebrate Thanksgiving. Even though I had grown up just over the George Washington Bridge, I had never seen the parade. It was Aileen's mantra, and it had prodded and inspired us many times before: The Crowley family was going to, in every way possible, be normal. And every few years, normal families in New Jersey make it into New York to see the Macy's Thanksgiving Day parade. So would the Crowleys. It would just mean traveling with a few more cars, people, pieces of equipment—and uncertainties—than the typical family. The three days in November that year were to be filled with memory-making opportunities: a Broadway show, shopping on Fifth Avenue, dinners out, a carriage ride around Central Park, and, of course, watching the parade.

The Crowley minivans pulled up to the Plaza Hotel in less than regal fashion. A silver Buick and a red Dodge minivan with handicapped hang-tags overloaded with people and medical equipment don't exactly trigger the New York paparazzi. (Try telling that to Megan.)

After having settled into our rooms, the Crowley Fun Machine began to roll. Megan broke out a map of Fifth Avenue stores and set about plotting her Wednesday afternoon "spree." It was to begin at the Disney store, three blocks south. Walt never envisioned a seven-year-old shopper as seasoned and savvy as Megan.

Aileen and I set out with John, Megan, and Patrick in tow. We had given them each a crisp $100 bill as "their money" to spend as they saw fit. Like ultramarathoners, we knew that we had to pace ourselves. John, always shy in public, stuck close to us. And we pushed Patrick's nonmotorized wheelchair, so that was not an issue. Megan, however, blazed her own path down the great shopping avenue in Manhattan. She had found her mecca. Her electric wheelchair was in turbo mode and she wasn't stopping until she reached the Disney store at Fifty-fifth Street and Fifth Avenue. You don't notice just how rough the sidewalks are, or how bumpy and uneven the handicapped street-crossing cutouts are, until you try to follow a seven-year-old Danica Patrick driving a 300-pound wheelchair.

Megan found the Disney Store in record time. After an hour of deliberate shopping, she proceeded to the checkout counter. The checkout girl rang up Megan's items (Barbie was her strong preference then), and the total came to $98. I was so proud of how Megan had calculated the amount of her purchases in her head to ensure that they came in under her allotted cash. I was overly optimistic in my assessment of her intentions.

Once the purchase total came up, I waited for Megan to reach for her purse, where she had secured the $100 bill I had given her an hour earlier. There was no visible movement. Not because she couldn't—Megan's arms worked just fine. Instead, she moved her eyes in my direction. At first the look said, "Daddy, did you not hear the young lady?" I waited. Megan glanced again. This time the look was more intense, more frustrated. It conveyed, simply, "Please put your right hand over your right butt cheek and pull out the small leather wallet with the magic plastic card, like you've done hundreds of times before." I sensed a negotiation. I uttered: "Megs, take your hundred-dollar bill and pay the nice young lady with *your* money." Megan's face registered the complete spectrum in quick succession, evolving from shock to grief to denial to amazement.

"Are you serious?" she finally asked.

"Yes, Megan, that's the deal," I rebuked her, proud of my father-knows-best tone. Begrudgingly, she complied. Megs is no brat, just a shrewd negotiator. I had won, for once. Aileen and I were feeling very satisfied. We had defined the limits of extravagance and maneuvered our special gang through the city with a certain deftness, even including Megan's chair getting stuck in the elevator and us having to pack into the cargo elevator to leave. For once, things were going our way. For once, a Crowley family outing may actually have been going according to plan.

The next day, I took John Jr. and Megan to visit my aunt. We were standing on the street corner and Megan kept nudging into my leg with her wheelchair. I looked down and told her to cut it out and she said, "I'm not doing anything." All of a sudden we realized a New York City bus that was making a wide turn had somehow latched its bumper onto Meg's chair. The bus started rolling and the next thing I knew it was pulling Megan down Fifth Avenue! I ran screaming down the street and caught up to the front and was pounding on the door as it rolled. Finally, the driver stopped the bus and we detached Megan's wheelchair.

The next morning, Thanksgiving Day, we woke the kids up early to get them ready to go to the parade. The parade travels from Manhattan's Upper West Side, around Columbus Circle, and down Seventh Avenue. The Plaza Hotel, where we were staying, is two avenues east of Columbus Circle. The daily ritual of waking Megs and Patrick, cleaning them, giving them an array of medicines and breathing treatments, dressing them, and getting them settled in their wheelchairs takes about two hours. By the time we got them settled in their chairs, it was going on 11:00 a.m. We never thought we would make it for the entire parade, but hoped to see as much as we could. Those hopes were quickly fading. The Crowley Fun Machine was in danger of being derailed.

By 11:20 we were on Central Park South opposite the Plaza Hotel. It was a blue-gray sky, brisk but not too cold. Perfect for parade watching. We could hear the music of a marching band, the sounds of helicopters buzzing overhead, and the sound of people. Lots of people. As we turned toward the west in the direction of the parade, we looked out at a sea of people. There were maybe a hundred yards ahead of us of relatively open space until the wall of people and police barricades. Aileen and I looked at each other and it hit us both at the same moment. Unlike at the Saint Patrick's Day parade, apparently you just couldn't saunter up and get a curbside view of *this* New York parade. Our Irish pride had told us that there was no way any parade in New York could ever be as popular and crowded as St. Pat's. We were wrong.

John Jr. was the first to ask the inevitable question: "How are we going to get up front and see the floats, Daddy?" We told him, "We will, just walk. Follow me." The Crowley family got about two blocks from Columbus Circle, where the action was, and... dead stop. There was no getting past the throngs of paradegoers. We told the kids to just look up to see some floats. Megan and Patrick sitting in their chairs, however, couldn't see anything above all the people in front of them. We were at a loss.

There was a blue NYPD police barricade adjacent to where we were standing. My mother-in-law, Kathy, moved toward it and asked the lieutenant standing there if she could move it just a few feet so her grandkids could see some floats in the distance. Without even looking, he said, in a tough Brooklyn accent, "Hey, lady, don't even think of moving that—" And then he stopped.

His eyes caught Patrick's. And then Megan's. His look, and posture, changed in an instant. He put on his police hat, tapped the two young patrolmen next to him, instructing them to move the barricade and "Let these nice people through." We looked up and a gigantic Bart Simpson loomed overhead. Patrick *really* liked that. That was very kind, and all we were expecting.

New York's Finest, though, weren't done helping these "nice people." The lieutenant, flanked by the two patrolmen, looked at us and said, "Follow me." For the next five minutes or so, he marched through the crowd, saying firmly, "Move. Make a hole. NYPD coming through. Get out of the way." At first, Aileen and I were a bit embarrassed by all the commotion and attention. The kids, however, shared no such discomfiture. They were on the move and with each minute they drew closer to a better view, closer to Santa's imminent arrival. We pressed on.

We got about a hundred feet from the parade line. Hundreds of people sat on the street enjoying the wonderful view that they had staked out, some as early as the evening before. The lieutenant instructed them to let these folks through. We were at the barricades. Not a soul stood between us and the high school band marching by. The noise was both deafening and exhilarating.

As we stopped, I turned to the cops to thank them. The lieutenant was looking at the kids and smiling. He noticed that the barricades themselves were at about eye level for Megan and Patrick. With the single motion of a cop long seasoned in New York, the lieutenant instructed the junior officers to move the barricades. They were immediately moved. We had arrived. We had the best view in New York.

I put my hand on the lieutenant's shoulder and said, "Thank you." He stood staring at the kids. Megs mouthed "thank you" to this tough cop from Brooklyn, and his eyes watered. Mine did, too. I told him, and the two patrolmen, that they had made our day. He just looked at Megs and Patrick and said, "No. They made mine. Happy Thanksgiving. God bless." And he turned and walked back to his post, the two patrolmen in tow.

Santa appeared just then, looked at the kids from his big float, not twenty feet away, and waved. This

Santa in a red suit made the trip for the kids—because another Santa in a blue suit with a gold badge gave them the chance. We could not do this for the kids without the help of these perfect strangers.

Part II

HOPE

CHAPTER 4

IT'S BIGGER THAN YOU

If I am not for myself, who will be?
If I am only for myself, what am I?
If not now, when? —Hillel the Elder

My last day at Bristol-Myers Squibb was Friday, March 24, 2000. I was leaving to begin work on what would become the treatment that saved my kids' lives. My first day at the new company was supposed to be Monday, March 27. But instead of reporting for duty as planned in Oklahoma, where the company was located, I decided to spend my first week on the new job in Boston.

Every year, there's a trade show in the biotech industry. It is referred to simply as "BIO." I now go most years to see what's going on in the industry. In 2000, at Boston's Hynes Convention Center, it was my first time—a "BIOVirgin" experience. I was a fly on the wall. I had a little nametag on and nobody knew who I was and nobody cared, and I didn't care to be known. I just wanted to listen, learn, and absorb.

Six months earlier, 40,000 anarchists had disrupted the World Trade Organization conference in what became known as the Battle of Seattle. For some reason, some of their sympathizers showed up in Boston in March 2000 to protest this biotech conference. As I checked into my hotel and saw the local news covering the protesters, I remember thinking, "This is odd. There are people walking around in skeleton suits and grim reaper costumes, holding up signs that say 'biotechnology executives = merchants of death.'" Strange, I kinda thought that biotechs made medicines that saved people's lives. Had I been led horribly astray?

The protesters dumped a vat of something on the front steps of the convention hall and the Boston Police called in the hazmat team. Everybody had to clear out of the convention hall spaces because they didn't know if it was a biological attack of some sort. It wasn't. It was plain old baked beans. I was looking at all this and thinking, "Gosh, what have I gotten myself into?" I had been in Big Pharma at Bristol-Myers Squibb, but this was all new to me. The biotech industry was just about twenty years old at that point; Genentech and Genzyme had been founded in the late 70s and early 80s.

I didn't get it. These companies, as well as the one I had cofounded, Novazyme, were about saving children and curing diseases. An apparent prerequisite to joining the anarchist crowd is having an awful lot of time on your hands. It turns out that the protests were aimed not at biotech but at agribusinesses, whose "crime" was to find ways to add more vitamins to rice to feed malnourished children in the developing world. This was my introduction to biotech. It was so much faster, more exciting, and more entrepreneurial than Big Pharma.

The keynote address at this convention was given by Christopher Reeve. There were thousands of people in the auditorium. When the curtain opened and he wheeled himself out, much of the audience was surprised by the extensive breathing apparatus he required, which was attached to his motorized wheelchair. But folks there were equally struck by the dignity and humility that he conveyed. Like any of us, he could speak only as he exhaled; the air being pushed out of our lungs is what powers the larynx. Just as with Megan and Patrick, Reeve's exhales were controlled by his ventilator, which gave his speech a halting rhythm. Still, it was fascinating to hear the strength in his voice, such a stark contrast in a man who couldn't move a muscle.

He spoke about the biotech industry. He said, "'Biotechnology' is a great big word. For people like me, it's got a simple definition. It's a great big word that means hope." It was incredibly inspiring. Reeve went on to tell the room that the work we were all doing holds incredible promise. He said that paralysis will absolutely be cured, and it will be the people in this room who cure it. He said that he hoped and prayed that such a cure will be developed in time to help him. But even if that wasn't to be, he said that there's a kid playing hockey somewhere in the Midwest who will fall and break his neck on the ice in the next few weeks. That teenager will be cured in ways that we in this room haven't even dreamed of today. And someday that kid will walk again. Or maybe that teenager isn't going to get hurt; it's his own kid who's going to get hurt twenty years from now. He told us, "As difficult as life can be for people who are paralyzed like I am, it's people like you in this room who give us some measure of hope."

It was so powerful to hear someone who had lost so much still brim with optimism for a hopeful future. I'm a faithful person. I believe that God has a daily impact in our lives. But there are those who look at Christopher Reeve and presume that God selected Christopher Reeve for paralysis "for a reason." I don't believe that. I don't believe that God manipulates our lives on such a granular level. I believe God helps to inspire people and gives them the tools to solve these very human problems.

People tell us all the time, "God must have picked you and Aileen to be the parents of Megan and Patrick because you have the patience or resources or love to care for them." I don't think so. If He did, I'm going to have a chat with Him when we get up there (very respectfully, mind you). And while not always blessed with great patience, I hope that I have had enough re-deeming moments in life that the scale tips somewhat in my favor on Judgment Day. I will certainly remind St. Peter about the Notre Dame–Michigan State game day in 2009. I wasn't watching John Jr. as closely as I should have been, and he ingested about 400 pounds of cotton candy at a pregame event. He was a tad "off," shall we say, the rest of the day. (Think Tasmanian devil on a mechanical bull, wildly slurping all the Red Bull he can get his hands on.) When we got home later that night from South Bend, I kidded with Aileen: "Someday, hopefully a long time from now, I'll be up at the pearly gates and St. Peter will be going through the list. Yes, that list. If he's got issues with some things I did in life—and I'm sure he will have many such issues— I'm going to play the video of today in South Bend." John was lit up like a Christmas tree but I was patient with him all day, uttering not a single foul word.

That's really what Christopher Reeve was getting at. I don't believe that we are assigned trials as opportunities to earn credit toward future paradise, and I don't believe we ought to search for ways to help simply as opportunities to gather "points." We hope for help with our own troubles. We hope for our loved ones. And we hope for those we'll never meet, no matter how much cotton candy they've had. That's what keeps us going.

After my kids first started taking the treatment for their Pompe, they showed incredible improvement. The immediate threat to their very lives was removed as the out-of-control enlargement of their hearts was brought back to normal. More than that, there was a period during which we could glimpse what their lives would be like if they didn't have Pompe disease. Not that they were running around in the yard and blow-ing saxophones. But in Megan especially, those few months where she was able to sit up by herself and watch television on the couch with me or lift her little 2-pound dumbbells while I worked out, that brief period was a gift from God for Aileen and me.

That gift was a constant reminder of the prize. We knew how meaningful our work to cure Pompe would be, even if a full cure arrived too late to benefit our kids. That gift was in my sights at all times.

Sometimes, I look back at the years I spent away from the kids, traveling back and forth to Oklahoma on fourteen hours of coach flights and transfers, and sleeping in the crappy little motel down the road from the start-up biotech company. I missed an awful lot of their growing up, and it put an incredible burden on Aileen. Had we failed, I might have felt very differently about chasing this particular miracle. We succeeded, at least to some degree. Working with many other people, we developed a treatment for Pompe that saved my kids' lives, and now is being taken by a thousand people living with Pompe all over the world. But just as important, we produced those special months when we glimpsed Megan and Patrick being able to do some of the things that normal kids do. It gave us hope and hope turned into courage and courage turned into strength.

Hope is an amazing commodity. My kids are alive because of the treatment that we helped to create. And because I've seen miracles, I have every reason to believe they will live happy lives for decades to come.

Maybe it's the technologies I'm working on at Amicus today or maybe new enzymes we haven't thought of yet. What Christopher Reeve was getting at is the uncanny way hope has of paying unexpected dividends. A kid playing with test tubes in a little science room we helped build at St. Paul's Catholic School in Princeton might grow up to get a Ph.D. and do something great.

That may sound far-fetched, but hope often defies logic. Some of the best-known discoveries in the history of medicine have been accidental. When scientists noticed that the high blood pressure medicine Loniten tended to slow or reverse balding, they started marketing its main ingredient, minoxidil, as Rogaine. A medication called sildenafil was ineffective at treating angina, but had the rather noticeable side effect of inducing profound penile erections. Viagra was born and life changed in a very pleasant way for a good many people.

That's how hope and inspiration work in tandem; it's bright people believing in the possibility of miracles. At that same biotech convention in Boston, Christopher Reeve shared another story. He had met some astronauts, and they gave him a signed poster and thanked him for being an inspiration to them. They were telling him that he was an inspiration to them and he was telling them the exact same thing. He told the audience of biotech scientists and executives that what we were working on right now is our country's next moon shot. In this room were the next Neil Armstrong and Buzz Aldrin and Sally Ride, who would do great things and inspire others to do great things. We would change the world.

Here was a man who had been at the apex of his field, a man of such strength that his most famous role was Superman. And he had lost the ability to move even the slightest muscle. Yet the audience could sense that he still held some small hope that he would hold on long enough for science to discover something that could help him. Christopher Reeve made it clear to everyone in that room that even if our efforts didn't help him, they wouldn't be for naught. It was going to be tough; it was going to take years. It may be like putting people on the moon. But it would be worth it. Even though it would likely be too late to help him, and maybe even to benefit anyone in that room, finding cures and relieving suffering are worth the effort because it elevates us all. That's how hope works.

America plays a unique role in manufacturing this type of hope. Just as America did with space travel, the U.S. gives rise to a particular type of individualism, entrepreneurship, capital, and philanthropy that all come together in this unique puzzle. Somehow the pieces fall in place and that often yields something just remarkable. It was true with the space program and it's been true in biotechnology. It's sometimes heartbreaking. It's never fast enough. But that little bit of hope, combined with an innate sense that anything is possible is a distinctly American form of cockeyed optimism.

Christopher Reeve died before doctors were able to repair his paralysis. But the fact that I heard that speech on the very first day of a career to which I have devoted my life shows the kind of impact one person's hope can have on another. That room was packed with people who spread out all over the world and worked a little bit harder, stayed a little bit later, to find ways to change the world.

What I heard that night has inspired me for almost a decade now. Stepping into the world of biotech and hearing that particular speech from that particular individual proves to me that God does play a role in our daily lives. He may not select who gets Pompe disease or which football team prevails (sorry, Notre Dame fans, not even in the case of the Fighting Irish). But He gives us the opportunities to contribute and do what we can to elevate our souls and improve the lives of those around us.

Accepting Kindness

After my dad died and we moved in with my grandparents, my mom took a job as a waitress at the Magic Pan at the Paramus Park Mall, and my grandfather kind of took on projects as they came. He was semiretired, so we didn't have any money. One day, my grandfather took my brother and me to lunch at one of the bars my dad and all his cop buddies used to visit in Englewood. It was a beautiful Sunday afternoon and we were just about to start eating our hot dogs when I looked up and saw a big jug on the bar. It was a big plastic jug that had originally held pretzels, and it was half-filled with dollar bills and change. On the front was a picture of my brother and me and it said, "Help the Crowley children."

My immediate reaction was, "Oh, that's really cool, our picture is on the bar." What Irishman wouldn't be proud to have his picture affixed to such an area of honor as a bar? Soon after, though, I was assaulted by a wave of embarrassment. I asked my dad's brother: "Uncle Jimmy, what's that for? We don't need that. We're okay, we've got an apartment, we've got food." Then, as soon as the thought formed, I began to worry: maybe we won't have a home, maybe we won't have food. Uncle Jimmy reassured me, "Oh no, John, that's just to help you guys out in the future, with college and stuff like that." There was probably fifty bucks in there.

That was thirty-five years ago, and it has stayed with me ever since—both the kindness of a tight-knit group like the police community and also the awkwardness, even at that young age, of being in a position to rely on the kindness of others.

It is very humbling to become the face of a cause. When we started raising money for Pompe research, it was one thing to say we were raising money for science, to build a department of research, or to fund a clinical trial. It was always easier to put it in that context rather than to say, "We need money for a project to save our own kids' lives."

When the kids were first diagnosed, my folks' neighbors in Norwood decided to put on a 5k run/ walk fundraiser to raise money. They are wonderful people, and they had only the purest motives. But when we got there, the runners' bibs had "Help Megan and Patrick" printed above big photos of the kids. They probably raised $1,000 that day. And again, it was remarkably kind and thoughtful of them, but it produced the same self-conscious, awkward feeling of having people pity us.

That happened again a few years later. We had grown accustomed to seeing people walk by us and put on what we've come to call the "cat smile." They see the wheelchairs and the ventilators and their expression says, "Oh, you poor dears." One day, we were pushing the kids to the arcade on the boardwalk in Ocean City, New Jersey, where we take our summer vacation. It was a beautiful night, and Megan liked to sip a small amount of water as she was pushed. So she had this little tin cup we'd fill with maybe a half-inch of water. All of a sudden, this fellow walking by dropped a quarter in her cup! Aileen and I were shocked, but Megan took it in perfect stride: "Cool, Daddy! Another quarter for the arcade!"

As jarring as that kind of experience can be, we have come to realize that it's a valuable part of the kids' lives. Megan and Patrick, by their very existence, provide an opportunity for others to do good.

In the Service of Others

One great way we can remind ourselves that there's more to life than our own provincial needs is through service to others.

My dad served four years in the Marines and a decade as a cop. My Uncle Jimmy was in the Navy before he became a cop. As a little kid, I'd go to the annual Englewood Police Day and see my dad on the motorcycle leading the parade. It made quite an impression. My heart would fill with pride as I watched my dad in his crisp uniform riding his shiny police motorcycle. My parents would take me to the National Guard Armory in Bergenfield to see the helicopters and the tanks. Without my dad ever saying, "You should do this because… ," I began to see a guy in a uniform and just admire the discipline, sacrifice, commitment, and service. He always knew "It" was bigger than him. Always.

I've tried to do the same as my parents did. Without forcing expectations on them, I've tried to teach my kids about service and sacrifice, community and patriotism. One way I've done that is to take John Jr. and a couple of nephews to Washington, D.C., every year for a boys' trip. There is no better backdrop to a theme of history, service, and sacrifice than our nation's capital.

I try to mix it up every year. The Air and Space Museum, Capitol Hill, the Spy Museum, but the one place we always visit is Arlington National Cemetery. It is the most hallowed ground in America. The first time we visited Arlington was in June 2003. I took John, then eight, and his cousin Connor, my oldest nephew at six years old. The Marine Corps Silent Drill Team and Band was playing at the Iwo Jima Memorial.

The Iraq war had just begun a couple of months earlier, and this was during the brief time where things looked like they were going reasonably well. At the ceremony, they were honoring two men, a Marine Corps general and a nineteen-year-old lance corporal whose leg had been amputated. I looked down and saw John Jr.'s attention darting around, looking at the flags and the band. He has attention-deficit hyperactivity disorder (ADHD) and it was in full swing.

We were standing up to show our respect, and I whispered to him, "John, do you know what they're talking about?" He replied in his mechanical way, "Yes, Daddy, I do. That young Marine there is a lance corporal. He served in the war against Saddam Hussein. He lost his leg. He got a Bronze Star and a Purple Heart. He's an American hero." I just looked at John and said, "You got it." I was never more proud of him. He got it in spades.

I've taught the kids that while war has incredibly honorable and heroic moments, it is not glorious or beautiful. War is awful, brutal, violent, and should be avoided whenever possible. It brings out the worst in man, but can also bring out the best. That night, in his own special way, John understood why we were all standing and paying our respects to this young man. He, too, knew it was bigger than him.

The next year, we went to the World War II Memorial for the first time. It's soaring and grand and incredibly moving. Once again, John Jr. was taking everything in, and when we got to the back of the Memorial, John pointed to the Field of Stars.

"Look at all those gold stars, Dad," he said.

"Yes, John, there are four thousand gold stars on this wall." I replied.

"That must be a gold star for every American killed in the war," he said.

"No, John," I said. "Each of those stars equals one hundred Americans killed in the war."

John got it immediately. He looked at the wall with this sense of awe and amazement and humility and stared for probably thirty seconds and didn't say a word, just walked on. It was different from the matter-of-fact way he had rattled off the particulars of the Gulf War medal recipients. But it carried equal impact. The look on his face and the respect shown by his silence said as much.

As a parent, you feel proud when your child reacts with depth and understanding to a fundamental value of your family. One of the objectives of raising a kid is to instill a sense of respect, sacrifice, and honor. So you feel proud that he gets it and hope that he'll internalize it throughout his life and teach others.

These values don't come out of nowhere. And they don't all come from parents, either.

People sometimes bemoan the lack of respect kids show for their country today. But because Aileen and I spend so much time in school with Megan and Patrick, we've gotten a very good view of something quite encouraging.

The principal of the John Witherspoon middle school in Princeton, Mr. Johnson, is right out of central casting: a tall, handsome, sixtyish African-American gentleman. He's a big, strong, no-nonsense guy, tough but sympathetic and loving. He also was a Marine Corps officer in the Vietnam era, which was fairly rare for African Americans. And every morning in Mr. Johnson's school, the Pledge of Allegiance is recited over the PA system. If Mr. Johnson is in the hall when it plays, he stands and recites it and he makes every kid in that hall stop and put their hands over their hearts. He and his fellow teachers at John Witherspoon set a standard of respect that kids see and want to emulate. They learn respect, they sense commitment, and they, too, get that it's bigger than them. It's about sacrifice for others more than it is about themselves. It's about giving of one's time, talent, and treasure.

That service doesn't, of course, come only from military service. There is a spirit of community and volunteerism that reaches every corner of the United States and touches every community. From churches, to schools, to programs for at-risk youth, we volunteer to help others, to make society stronger and more just. Aileen and I tell our nieces and nephews that we don't care if they serve in the Peace Corps or the Marine Corps when they are older, but that they should serve somewhere and somehow. That notion of service to others is another cornerstone of our uniquely American heritage and culture. It's part of what makes this nation so very strong and so very special. It reminds us that America is not just some random land on a globe, but a place in our hearts, minds, and souls.

Marriage

Maintaining perspective on our marriage became critical after the kids' health challenges began to consume our family's every thought. The strain this can place on a marriage is difficult to convey. The fear and sadness you both feel for your kids is all-consuming. On top of that fear and sadness is the fact that there's little time to work on the husband-and-wife issues that all couples face. In the six months between the fall of 1998 and the early spring of 1999, Aileen and I grew dangerously apart. Life wasn't supposed to be this way. During that time, Megan almost died from cardiac and respiratory failure, spending six weeks in an ICU and finally coming home attached to a respirator. Then a few months later, we went through it all again with Patrick. We wish we had had the wisdom and strength then that we have now. We would have saved a lot of self-inflicted pain. It was overwhelming, and we both regret those dark days. We regret mostly the things we said and did to each other, most of which I admit were wholly my fault.

Divorce rates are staggeringly high among parents of special needs children, with some studies suggesting that 85 percent of these couples don't make it. Like all married couples, Aileen and I have had our moments of crisis, dark periods where we couldn't be sure our marriage would survive. But we didn't want to be another sad story. Not only because our children needed us, but because we knew that underneath the struggles we were facing, there was a deep well of love and respect and joy and shared goals and all the other strengths that good marriages need to survive. Sometimes, it's simply a matter of allowing those feelings to shine through.

A marriage is bigger than one person. For parents of kids with very special needs, those needs can consume all their time, energy, and even love. It's critical to keep your marriage strong. For the parents' sake, to have a partner as you confront difficult challenges. But also for the kids' sake. Children with special needs are often keenly aware of the added responsibilities their parents face. Aileen and I have made it a point to make time for our marriage.

One goal I mentioned earlier is that we try to have a date each week, or at least every other week. We get dressed up somewhat and go to dinner and try to discuss grown-up topics and the world beyond central New Jersey, sometimes even heading to New York for a late dinner or a show. We used to do this fairly easily when the kids were younger. Megan and Patrick would go to bed at 7:00 and had a nurse with them, so as long as John Jr. was accounted for, we were able to sneak out by 8:00. If we didn't go out, we'd at least get dressed up and, instead of sitting at the kitchen table, eat in the dining room and light candles.

This rule about having dates didn't come out of nowhere. We learned a long time ago that if we don't make time for each other, then nothing else falls into place. For the first two years after the kids were diagnosed with Pompe disease, there was no "Aileen and John" whatsoever. Our entire lives were spent caring for the kids, managing the nurses, and developing a treatment.

At some point in the early days of caring for the kids, we looked up and realized we were drifting apart as a couple. We were not happy with each other. I didn't think she was running the house with perfect efficiency, and she was fed up with my criticism and constant absence. It got to the point where Aileen was ready to kick me out, and I was ready to leave.

It was the culmination of a lot of little things. I wanted life to be different. Over time, I had begun to rationalize and told myself that we'd all be better off if Aileen and I lived separately, perhaps even next door so I could continue to be involved with the children as much as possible, but not as man and wife. The intense time when Megan got so sick and almost died and then the same happened to Patrick was all-consuming and occurred in less than six months. And for Aileen and me as individuals, dealing with emotions differently, it all intensified by an order of magnitude. You say things and do things and go places that in another world you probably wouldn't.

Like many couples, we struggled to communicate. I like to talk a lot more than Aileen, maybe sometimes too much. And maybe sometimes Aileen likes to talk too little. It's important to me to lay it out there and be blunt and not pretend things are okay when they're not. And I want Aileen to do the same, but she is more likely to internalize her feelings. And then she'll say, "Please don't lecture me." And it does sometimes run into a lecture because when she doesn't want to talk, I'll offer my ten suggestions on how to make life better. And she'll just look at me as if to say, "What a pain in the ass."

The few times we've ever actually had an argument, it's always ended the same way. I'll ask her why she won't discuss something and she'll make reference to my days on the Notre Dame moot court team: "Well, it's not particularly pleasant going up against the captain of the freaking debate team."

It was a very tough time, and I think that one particular night it just kind of reached a peak. In some ways, I suppose I wanted to force a confrontation, because Aileen never fights, never argues, never confronts. When I told her I had had it and was walking out, Aileen played tough. "Okay, good luck. Have fun with that," she said sarcastically. I hung around a bit longer and said, "I'm really leaving now." I wanted her to just reach out and grab me and say, "No, you're right. This is what we have to do, and it will all be okay." She didn't. And that pissed me off even more. Finally, I said, "I'm really leaving now." She didn't even turn her head from the television set. She just said, "Okay, drive safely. Let me know when you want to come back."

I drove and drove, and as I did, I thought about the fights my mother and stepfather would have when we were kids. My stepfather, Lou, was always good to my brother and me. But his relationship with my mother grew quite strained over the years. Sometimes he'd move out of the house for a week; other times he'd be gone for six months. Through it all, my mom always worked hard to keep us together and strong. She sacrificed immensely for our future. And my stepfather, though now divorced from my mom, has made peace with my brother and me and has been a wonderful grandfather to our kids.

As I drove, I thought about what those fights had done to my brother and me, how jarring they had been to our sense of security. I thought about how, underneath the frustrations and slights, I loved Aileen more deeply than ever. We had been through some of the hardest challenges parents can face and I knew that we still loved each other, not just as partners in the care of our children but as adults who were still just plain crazy about each other. At the end of the day, as I sped north toward who knows where, I couldn't imagine growing old without Aileen.

I came back at 4 a.m. the next morning. I got into bed and lay next to Aileen and I kissed her and said, "I love you," and she said very matter-of-factly, "I love you, too."

Later, Aileen told me, "We're struggling with every ounce of our beings to save the kids' lives. But if we don't save our family, we're not going to have the happy kids and happy family we're working to save. We can get angry and frustrated and storm out of the house. Neither one of us wants that. Or we can work on this."

So that's what we did. We just wanted to make things work, and it is "work." Enjoyable, wonderful, rewarding work, but it is work, and it doesn't simply happen. You have to make it a priority. We agreed to make time to be together, not just for dates, but to commit to quiet time at night for fifteen minutes and occasional three-day weekends away.

Aileen asked me to make an effort to be home more, to stop saying yes to every possible meeting, running to even the remotest location on the chance of raising a few dollars or generating a new idea for a cure. I started to create rituals with each of the kids—taking John Jr. to school or putting Megan to bed—so that I wouldn't suddenly notice that weeks had elapsed without having seen Aileen or the kids awake.

That was ten years ago. I'm not going to claim that living with me has been an uninterrupted pleasure for Aileen ever since; I assure you it has not. But I will say that she and I have worked hard to find balance and to remember the other's needs. Once when I was in Tampa for Navy Reserve training in 2008, I called home to say hello and I described the oppressive heat and humidity. I asked what it was like in New Jersey. Aileen told me it had been a "pretty nice day." Later that evening, I spoke to someone from work, and he happened to mention that it had rained all day and there was a thunderstorm warning. Aileen wasn't fibbing. That's just how she sees the world: "Nothing's a problem and everything's twenty minutes away."*

---

*There's a funny story about one of Aileen's rare efforts to engage in confrontation. There was a snowstorm on a Friday night a couple of years ago, and it's always tough for us because we live on this tiny little side street off a winding, hilly road. We are literally the last ones plowed after a snowfall, and if it's not plowed, the nurses can't make it up the steep hill. This one storm a few winters ago was very severe and it was taking a long while. Aileen was growing more and more concerned and told me, "This is ridiculous. I am calling the township." I tried telling her, "Honey, I don't think anybody is there at night. If they are, they are probably out driving the trucks." That only annoyed her more. She is sweet and easygoing and has the gentlest personality. Until she gets her "Irish" fired up—then watch out. So she called the Department of Public Works and was on hold and just kept tapping her foot, growing increasingly annoyed.

She looked over at me and mouthed, "I got the machine." Finally, she said, "This is Aileen Crowley. My street is currently not paved. It is 11:15 in the evening on Friday. As you know, we have two children with very special needs and we have nurses who need to get up our street. It is *absolutely imperative* that my street be paved. Immediately. If my street is not paved in the next two hours…" And I'm trying to get her attention to let her know that she's not using the right verb, and she's looking at me and the "just a minute" finger keeps going up, as if to say, "I will deal with you in a second, Mr. Pushy—I'm handling this." So I just kind of lean back and let her go, and she is lit. This is as stern a message as she's left a human being in her life. Finally, she concludes,

It's a lovely way to look at life. Abundant optimism. Our marriage is a blessing, and I am forever grateful for that Halloween party back in 1984.

"Good day, sir," and hangs up.

She looks at me and I just start giggling and she says, "What? What's so freaking funny?" I reply, "I'm just thinking about the chuckle the guy is going to get when he shows up at 9:00 on Monday morning and checks the messages and hears about the crazy woman at the top of the hill who emphatically insists that the Department of Public Works in Princeton Township come out in a snowstorm and *pave* her road. Immediately!"

Aileen's face turns bright red and she unleashes a string of choice words on me, this time selecting each one with the precision that had eluded her while leaving the phone message.

CHAPTER 5
RISK AND INNOVATION

Do not go where the path may lead, go
instead where there is no path and leave a
trail.—Ralph Waldo Emerson

I left the comfort of the Bristol-Myers Squibb Company in March 2000 for the unknown world of leading a four-person biotechnology start-up company in Oklahoma with no revenue, no product, and an untested idea that would require years to prove. It was as start-up as start-ups get. At some point early on, quite frankly, it seemed more like start-down than start-up. But we were innovators on a mission, a mission where failure was not an option. We bootstrapped the company from day one. We would buy used scientific equipment—centrifuges, incubators, microscopes, refrigerators—on a sort of eBay for lab equipment.

It was very different than my previous life in corporate America. At Bristol-Myers, if there was a computer problem, I'd call the IT department and our own geeks on call would rush to the rescue. At my start-up, if the computer went down, I was the geek. I had taken a significant pay cut and our nascent company was still running out of money. I borrowed money to help make ends meet and cashed in a small 401(k) savings account. At one point, we were down to $37,000 in the business, which was about ten days' worth of cash flow. Just about eighteen months later, we sold that company for well over $100 million and ultimately contributed toward developing the treatment that saved our kids' lives.

The story of medical breakthroughs is one of risk and innovation. The story of the biotech industry is one of extreme risk and astounding innovation. And when it works, it reaches remarkable success, the kind of success that is defined on many levels. Some of the greatest risk taking and greatest successes have been in the field of rare genetic disease drug development.

One Mom Can Change the World

In the United States, the Rare Disease Act of 2002 defines "rare disease" strictly according to prevalence, as "any disease or condition that affects less than 200,000 persons in the United States." Other countries have different standards, but the basic idea is that a rare disease is one wherein the average general practitioner would not see it in more than one patient per year. There are approximately 7,000 rare diseases in the world. Before 1983, drugs had been approved for only about a dozen of those diseases. One woman changed all that.

Abbey Meyers was a housewife from Connecticut, who later would found the National Organization for Rare Disorders (NORD). One of her sons had Tourette's syndrome. While most people associate Tourette's with the uncontrolled exclamation of obscenities—comedians and Hollywood writers love to portray people with Tourette's spewing curse words randomly—the truth is that only a small fraction of people living with Tourette's actually make such utterances. For most, it is a disease of sudden and repetitive movements, or tics. In 1983 there were no drugs available specifically for Tourette's, but a schizophrenia drug called pimozide had shown a lot of promise in treating her son, who was taking it in a clinical trial.

Unfortunately, pimozide failed to show much benefit for the schizophrenia sufferers for whom it was primarily intended. In 1980, McNeil Laboratories pulled the plug on this "orphan drug" because Tourette's didn't provide a big enough market to justify the expense of developing it. The risk of spending all that money to develop a drug was not sustainable, since most drugs fail and the few that don't can be easily copied by other pharmaceutical companies.

More than 25 million Americans today live with a rare disease, a number that dwarfs far better-known diseases. But one of the problems in attracting attention to rare diseases is that no one of them has many sufferers. Few people had heard of Tourette's syndrome at the time that pimozide was being abandoned. Abbey started to talk to people whose lives had been affected by other rare diseases. One of those people was Marjorie Guthrie, the widow of Woody Guthrie, who had died of Huntington's disease.

Abbey started to put together trips to Washington, where family members could educate Congress about the orphan drug problem: With profits dependent on the size of the market rather than the medical needs of patients, drugmakers couldn't be persuaded to invest in treatments for rare diseases. One Congresswoman, Elizabeth Holtzman, introduced a bill to try to help, but it didn't address the root of the problem.

Abbey Meyers recognized the need to create market incentives for drugmakers to develop drugs aimed at much smaller patient markets. She approached Congressman Henry Waxman and found a sympathetic ear, but throughout the early 1980s they couldn't generate much attention. One day, they got a break. Abbey had brought a gentleman named Adam Seligman to testify. There was virtually no one in the room besides Congressman Waxman and his staff. But a reporter from the *LA Times* happened to be there, and he wrote a story about Seligman traveling to Canada to get a drug that wasn't available in the United States, only to have it confiscated by border agents on the way home.

A fellow named Maurice Klugman read that story and called Abbey. He was a producer of the television show *Quincy*, which starred his brother Jack Klugman as a medical examiner with a mission. Maurice Klugman produced an episode of *Quincy* about Tourette's, based on the Seligman story. At the end, a public service announcement explained that the problem portrayed in the episode was real and invited viewers to write to the show if they wanted to help solve the problem of orphan drugs for rare diseases.

Thousands did. All of a sudden, the issue was attracting the attention that had eluded Abbey and others who had worked so hard over the years. Jack Klugman went to Capitol Hill to advocate for a draft bill of what became the Orphan Drug Act. Klugman told the lawmakers, "I'm not trying to legislate morality. Just encourage it."

The next season, *Quincy* aired another episode on rare diseases, this time featuring the character going to Washington to meet the fictional senator who was standing in the way of this Orphan Drug Act. It was a case of art imitating life.

In one scene, Jack Klugman is in the senator's office. He says something like, "Senator, you don't realize how important this is to people. There are masses of people in the United States who want this, those who have no voice." And he opened the window to reveal thousands of people in wheelchairs marching on the mall in Washington.

I remember the fictional senator saying, "Well, Doctor, I can't support your legislation, but I won't stand in the way." That episode, which aired on October 27, 1982, prompted the real-life politicians to action. With bipartisan support, the Orphan Drug Act was signed into law on January 4, 1983. It would provide market incentives, such as seven years of market exclusivity, to makers of drugs for rare diseases. That bill led to an entire new subset of the biotech and pharmaceutical industry focusing on rare disorders. When Reagan signed that bill in a ceremony at the White House, he said, "I only wish with the stroke of this pen I could also decree that the pain and heartache of people who suffer from these diseases would cease."

It hasn't ceased yet, but we are on our way. Not even thirty years later there are now more than 330 drugs approved for hundreds of rare diseases—some of them cures, some palliatives, some falling somewhere in the middle, like the one we developed for Pompe. Without the Orphan Drug Act, none of these advancements would have been possible. With the support of Jack Klugman, and the vision and passion of Abbey Meyers, the world is a better place. Taken together, all rare diseases in the United States are more prevalent than HIV and all cancers combined—millions of voices longing to be heard, to be cured, and, above all, to be respected. Not so "rare" after all. Oh, and that last *Quincy* episode was titled, appropriately, "Give Me Your Weak."

One Company Can Save a Life

Genzyme Corporation is a remarkable story of bio-tech success. Without the Orphan Drug Act, Genzyme would not have been able to develop its breakthrough drug for Gaucher disease (a rare genetic disorder), a drug now known as Cerezyme. And without Cerezyme, there likely would never have been a drug for Pompe.

Genzyme's drug for Gaucher patients was originally being developed in an earlier form at the National

Institutes of Health by Dr. Roscoe Brady. There was also another doctor, Robin Berman, who had several children with Gaucher. She had advocated for the NIH to do this research, and they did a study in a small number of patients and it failed in all but one patient. After that, she helped arrange for Genzyme to pick it up. Henry Blair at Genzyme had a vision that a couple of dozen people in the company would take this drug and refine it based on the results from the one young child it helped.

This one kid, Brian Berman (one of Robin's children), had shown an improvement in his spleen volume, the most manifest symptom of the disease. Genzyme scientists went back and modified the particular characteristics of this enzyme therapy and put it back in another twelve-person clinical study with enzyme derived from human placental tissues. This was as creative as anyone in the field had ever been, especially after such discouraging initial results and such a small potential market for the drug. Most biotech companies would have given up.

Genzyme executives, led by their visionary CEO Henri Termeer, went to the FDA to explain how they were going to make this drug for maybe 2,000 people in the world. He told them how he would produce the drug from discarded placentas, collected after births in Europe, and that approximately 20,000 purified placentas *per patient* were needed to produce enough treatment *per year*. Basically, every placenta in France for a couple of years went to make enzymes for the small number of people with Gaucher disease. It was an incredibly innovative process. It was beyond risky, on the outer boundary of the intersection where business and science meet.

The FDA thought Genzyme was nuts. They'd never make money on it, the company would go out of business, and people with Gaucher would be back where they began.

In that second twelve-person study, however, the clinical results were incredible. The treatment worked beautifully. Genzyme essentially created a cure for most people with Gaucher. The before and after photos leave no doubt that the effort was worth the risk. Prior to treatment, young kids had spleens so bloated that they looked as though they were nine months' pregnant. Their bones were weak, their gums were bleeding, many couldn't get out of bed. Photos of them two to three years later show them no different from unaffected children, as close to a medical miracle as possible.

In the meantime, Genzyme realized there were far more people with this disease than had been believed. They realized they could have a much bigger product on their hands if they could produce the treatment in greater quantity, using bioreactors in a more standard biotech process. In the mid-1990s, Genzyme built a $200 million plant on the Charles River in Boston, right across from Harvard Business School.

Our family watched them build it because our home while I attended Harvard Business School looked down on that plant. When Megan was born in the spring of my second year at HBS, I used to rock her to sleep out on our patio overlooking the Genzyme plant, across from the HBS parking lots. I didn't know what Genzyme was, and at the time I quite frankly couldn't have cared less. We used to call it the "Willy Wonka" plant because we never really saw people coming in or out during the day. We suspected that little orange "oompa loompas" worked there at night. Little did we know that one day that exact cutting-edge biologics manufacturing plant would be where much of the drug for Pompe disease would eventually be made, including the drug that would save Megan and Patrick.

That combination of risk—pursuing a drug that had already failed—and innovation, in creating an almost implausible biologics manufacturing process, gave birth to one of the biggest biotech companies in the world. There are now eight drugs approved for six different lysosomal storage disorders, such as Gaucher, Fabry, and Pompe, with four more in clinical development. Every one of them has its roots in that first success, and every one is aimed at treating diseases with very small patient populations. If you had ever written that in a business plan—take a failed drug for a tiny market and make it by finding 20,000 placentas per patient per year in France—people would have thought you were nuts. But if Genzyme hadn't taken that risk, my kids and thousands of others would not be alive today.

The early search to identify and cure Pompe itself is also a story of risk and innovation.

Johann Pompe was a Dutch pathologist who had done his Ph.D. work describing a disease that caused a small number of Dutch babies to be born with enlarged hearts and floppy muscles. He characterized it as a glycogen-storage disease and dedicated his lab to it. He also served in the Dutch resistance during World War II. When the Nazis discovered a radio transmitter in his lab, Dr. Pompe was executed and his lab was burned down. No one did a thing for Pompe disease for the next twenty-five years.

In the early 70s, the first-ever enzyme replacement therapy was tried. As Dr. Roscoe Brady would attempt years later for Gaucher, the Pompe researchers took enzyme derived from human placenta, purified it, and infused it in the cells of two infants suffering from a very severe form of the disease. They continued the infusion for a month or two, but both babies died. The study was an abject failure.

The scientists saw those results and basically concluded that enzyme replacement therapy doesn't work. A decade later, a doctor named Stuart Kornfeld, at Washington University in St. Louis, thought again about their method. He characterized the trafficking pathways for how those enzymes are made naturally within our bodies, how they are transported naturally, and he identified the carbohydrates and sugars involved. He theorized that the problem with the earlier enzyme replacement therapy was that when the enzymes were taken from human placenta, the sugars had already been cleaved off, so only protein and no sugars remained. His theory was that enzyme replacement therapy would work but would need very specific protein with the sugars attached.

With normal enzymes, the first thing the enzymes do is strip the sugars, which are really just there for trafficking. Dr. Kornfeld's innovation was to identify the trafficking pathway and to realize that the right sugars had to be attached. That's why Genzyme's first trial failed: They didn't have the right sugars arranged in the pattern necessary for each lysosomal storage disorder. The reengineered sugars were critical to the success Genzyme eventually had with Gaucher.

By the 1980s, doctors at Duke and in the Netherlands were identifying some of the genes specific to Pompe. It would still take more than another decade, and investments of hundreds of millions of dollars, to bring the first drug for Pompe to people living with the disease.

Fast forward to today, and we realize even more intensely that these treatments require constant innovation. In January 2003, when I first pressed the button to give Megan and Patrick their enzyme at the hospital, I thought we were done. We had climbed a mountain to develop the treatment and gone through rings of fire to get it to our kids. And pressing that button and seeing it drip into Megan and Patrick seemed like a golden chalice had been delivered. This was going to solve everything. And then as I saw the kids quickly progress, it seemed even more clear that the treatment had worked as intended. Especially with Megan, it really did take on the appearance of a miracle. She would lift those two-pound dumbbells with me and sit up by herself, just six months after being barely able to move.

Over the course of the first half of 2004, we began to realize just how much work remained. The treatment was a good start. It fixed their hearts and made them stronger for a while. It was a very positive move forward for people living with Pompe, but it's certainly not the final answer. That's when I realized we needed to innovate constantly and to think about next-generation approaches to treating the disease. The need for constant innovation is certainly true in rare diseases. It's true in all medicine. I think it's true in any industry. The treatment that Megan and Patrick received shrank their dangerously oversized hearts and kept them alive. Taking that risk bought us and others working in the rare genetic diseases field the time to continue to innovate, to dream of the next discoveries and inventions that would move us forward in the quest to extend and enhance people's lives. To decree, in a way, "that the pain and suffering of people living with these conditions [s]hould cease."

Risk, When It's Personal

Judging when to take a medical or scientific risk is complicated when you run a biotech company. It's even more complicated when you're a dad.

Megan and Patrick never put any weight on their bones, which has led to their bones growing very brittle and fragile. On X ray, their arms look as thin as chicken bones, and they're highly susceptible to fracture. Pompe disease doesn't exactly cause this, but it's a secondary effect not uncommon in neuromuscular diseases.

Several doctors, including our old friend Dr. Slonim, had been recommending a bone infusion treatment, wherein a drug is injected and binds to bone to enhance bone strength. The goal is the same as those produced by the blockbuster bone-strengthening drug Boniva, but instead of a once-a-day pill, it's administered as a powerful infused medicine called Reclast. The treatment is generally given to older people with very severe osteoporosis.

We'd been delaying a decision on this because the kids have so many doctors and medical treatments as it is. And it's not an easy procedure. They couldn't find anything in the literature about this drug being given to a child. The only doctor on the East Coast willing to administer this drug was at Morgan Stanley Children's Hospital at Columbia Presbyterian in Manhattan. Just getting the kids in and out of a hospital in New York is a logistical ordeal, kind of like arranging for the pope to come to town. It would require three to five visits each before the infusion to complete the bone scans that tell the doctor how to infuse. Since it's given only once or twice a year, we thought it might be worth the hassle, but we weren't certain. Then, in the summer of

2009, Patrick's arm just snapped as he was being put in his wheelchair. We finally decided to move forward with the treatment.

I took Megan in one van and Aileen took Patrick in the other and the Crowley Fun Machine began to roll. Naturally, it was pouring rain as we motored over the George Washington Bridge and pulled up to the hospital, "Crowley's Law" being in full force and effect. There's a big sign that reads "Morgan Stanley Children's Hospital" and below that in little letters, it says "At Columbia Presbyterian Medical Center." Megan's eyesight is not that great, so all she saw was "Morgan Stanley." She began shouting, "Dad, this isn't a hospital. This is a bank!" It took all of her self-control not to utter "you moron" in the middle of her sentence. I couldn't help but chuckle, and also admire my little trouper's good brain (she'd seen Morgan Stanley's name on our bank statements). Judging by the strength of her objection, she seemed subliminally suspicious of a hospital funded by a bank that had taken bailout money. I assured her that this was a hospital—a great one, in fact—and that it was solvent and reputable. She acquiesced and we parked.

Parking was the easy part. Administering to the kids their next novel medicine would prove tougher. Both Megan and Patrick have ports implanted in their chests. Their vasculature is so weak that you can't just stick them with needles. We had these infusion ports installed for the kids to get their enzyme replacement treatments, and the ports last about five years. They're each on their second one now.

Actually, even installing those ports was an ordeal, and Patrick almost didn't make it. To install a port, they open up the chest with a big incision and then snake the line up into the jugular. From there, it goes down into one of the veins that feed directly into the heart, so that the treatment goes right into the vasculature. When Patrick was getting his installed at five years old, they wouldn't let Aileen into the operating room, so she stood outside the room for hours. They were having a very tough time getting Patrick's installed and his blood pressure dropped so low that he nearly died on the table. When the surgeon finished, he saw Aileen standing outside and angrily said, "I hope what you just made me do to that baby was worth it."

Anyway, we thought that having the ports would at least make the infusion easier, but because of the length of these needles and because of potential complications of this treatment, it takes quite a bit of skill even to perform the infusion through the port. So they sent us to the Pediatric Oncology Unit, which has the highest level of expertise for kids who are "tough sticks" (as in, tough to get a needle into). Of course, that block-and-a-half walk triggered its own mini-adventure. It's pouring and I've got Megan and we somehow turned down the wrong street, and Aileen and the kids' head nurse, Sharon, are calling my cell and screaming, "How the heck do you get lost walking down the block?" Megan and I were engrossed in conversation and lost our way. Typical for us.

We finally make it in to the infusion center and the kids spend an hour or so getting their blood pressures and other vitals taken. A Pediatric Oncology unit is tough. If you ever need perspective in life, visit a kids' oncology unit. You realize instantly how lucky you are. Kids from age two to thirteen, most of them bald, are sitting there getting chemotherapy. Megan and Patrick really can't sit up, so they had a bed in a little side area of the very large infusion room. Of course, they had pooped, so we had to change them as well. These pediatric oncology nurses see plenty, but they weren't accustomed to seeing a whole road crew like the Crowley Fun Machine. Literally, that's how we roll.

In addition to the usual suspects, the Crowley crew had an extra member. Dr. Alfred Slonim was not just one of the world's foremost expert in Pompe disease and a professor of pediatrics at Columbia, he has also become a personal friend of the family. Dr. Slonim's presence set off a tizzy among the nurses who were wondering why such a prominent physician would be hanging around for a lengthy period of time.

Alfred Slonim is an Orthodox Jew born and raised in Australia, where he played Australian football before moving to Israel and fighting in the wars of 1967 and 1973. Soon after, he went to Vanderbilt University, and in the hills of Appalachia he met a family with several Pompe children, which is how he got into the field. Dr. Slonim met Megan and Patrick at the beginning of our journey with Pompe in 1998. He was the first person to give us even a glimmer of hope.

The nurses started with Patrick first, and I was concerned because he's always so sensitive, but the nurse was very good and got it on the first try. She hit the port with the needle, and it went right into his chest and he didn't even flinch.

We breathed a sigh of relief when we saw the blood coming back through the needle, the indication that a solid connection has been established. Megan is often a harder stick than Patrick because her scoliosis has twisted her little body. I told Megan, "See, honey, it's no problem. These ladies are professionals, and all they do is access ports all day long."

I stayed with Patrick for about half an hour and was talking to him and catching up with Dr. Slonim, when all of a sudden we heard this awful wail. I ran to Megan's bed and I saw her lying there, tears flowing down and she was shaking. She never cries like that, never. The nurse was trembling and she said, "We can't get the stick." They had tried twice, basically as if Megan were being jabbed inside her chest with a long, thick needle. I held her hand and tried to comfort her, but she just kept repeating, "No, I want out of here. NOW. Please, Daddy, please!"

She was in agony. They brought in a nurse who was apparently the expert of the whole unit. I said to her, "I guess you drew the short straw." And we said to Megan, "This nurse is the total pro. Give it one last chance, and if it doesn't work, Megs, that's it."

She wouldn't hear of it. This is so unlike Megan, our toughest kid. So I can only imagine how painful these failed attempts were. We told her, "Honey, you need this medicine." And she was just hysterical, crying uncontrollably when they stuck her again—and again it failed. Aileen and I had told her this third attempt would be the last. But the head nurse felt positive that if she changed to a shorter needle that she could get it to take. We begged Megan to let us try just one more time. She agreed. Thank God, this time it worked.

It took us about ten minutes to calm her down. The nurse was getting all set, and I had my hand under Megan's head while the nurse put this big butterfly of tape over the needle to keep it in place. It looked like it was about to come out, and Megan shot me this laser-beam scowl that told me, "If this damn thing comes out, there's no way I'm letting you put it back in." The best way to calm Megan down is to tell her about John Jr.'s misadventures. I described to her how John and I had been in Washington the previous weekend and saw Old Glory, the actual flag that inspired "The Star-Spangled Banner." I told Megan how John Jr. had pointed and said, "This is why Scott Francis Key wrote the national anthem." She relishes his dyslexia. Cannon fodder for her pointed wit.

So it was an ordeal, but a few minutes later Megan was looking out into the room to the open area filled with kids getting infused. Some of them are pretty sickly kids. But it was Megan and Patrick who garnered most of the attention because of their unique physical limitations, heavy load of equipment, and near–rock star entourage. Heck, they can't even sit up, and they have experimental medicine pouring through permanent holes in their chests. Megan has just been through holy hell for the last hour and a half. She motions for me to come close so no one can hear and says, in her crazy little ventilator voice, "Dad, do you see all those kids over there? They all have cancer. I feel so bad for those kids. That is so not fair."

Dr. Slonim was standing there at the end of her bed. He was leaning against the wall, and he just looked at me and said almost under his breath, "Remarkable." That's Megan. Remarkable, indeed. And she and Patrick and many others like them have paved the way for the advancements to come. They have given more than they will ever receive. They are among the central actors on the stage of innovation in medical science today.

In the next twenty to thirty years I truly believe that we will diagnose, treat, and probably cure just about all genetic diseases. Most cancers will be cured and others will be treated as a long-term, manageable chronic condition. If somebody had said 150 years ago that we will soon double the life span of human beings, that nobody was going to die of polio or tuberculosis or scarlet fever, that if someone got an infection, he wouldn't automatically suffer and die—no one would have believed it.

I envision a day where a pregnant woman who needs to be informed exactly what metabolic issues her baby may face, Pompe disease or some formerly fatal neurodegenerative disorder, can at the same time be reassured that there's a pill or a therapy available to correct it. There are major ethical issues surrounding these eventualities, and we will need to address them frankly and with open minds. To the extent that we can extend and enhance and fundamentally improve the quality of life, however, we may soon be able to "cure" the aging process itself. Imagine the possibilities.

In the biotech industry, our duty as entrepreneurs, scientists, and doctors is to find the best medicines and the best treatments that we can for the human race. God has given us many of the tools, the understanding of His creation, and the inspiration to act. Now we have to harness this power, and harness it for the betterment and advancement of all humankind. As a society, we have to develop guidelines about how best to use those tools. In the very near future, we will have a whole host of health issues to deal with that we can't even dream of today. At the same time, we will have made a lasting contribution for generations to come. The combination of risk and innovation has truly introduced a new golden age of medicine. This is our hope; this will be our legacy.

Chapter 6

SET A VISION AND DREAM BIG

> *Few will have the greatness to bend history itself; but each of us can work to change a small portion of events, and in the total of all those acts will be written the history of this generation.*—*Robert F. Kennedy*

In 1980, seven-year-old Chris Greicius was being treated for leukemia. Every day, he dreamed of becoming a police officer. U.S. Customs Officer Tommy Austin had befriended Chris and his mother, Linda Bergendahl-Pauling. He promised Chris a ride in a police helicopter. When Chris's health worsened, Austin contacted Ron Cox, an Arizona Department of Public Safety officer, and planned a day that would lift Chris's spirits.

On April 29, 1980, Austin and a caring group of DPS personnel started Chris's day with a tour of the city in a department helicopter, which also flew him to headquarters. Three cruisers and a motorcycle officer greeted him before his meeting with the DPS command staff. There, Chris was sworn in as the first honorary DPS patrolman in state history.

But his experience didn't stop there. Cox contacted John's Uniforms, which agreed to make a custom-tailored DPS uniform for Chris. The owner and two seamstresses worked through the night to finish it. The officers presented the official uniform to Chris on May 1 and arranged a motorcycle proficiency test so he could earn wings to pin on his uniform. Chris passed the test with flying colors on his battery-operated motorcycle.

On May 2, Chris was back in the hospital. He asked to arrange the room so he could always see his uniform, his motorcycle helmet, and his Smokey Bear–style campaign hat. DPS motor officer Frank Shankwitz presented Chris with his motorcycle wings. He accepted them with a smile that lit up the room. The following day, Chris passed away.

But with this wonderful experience was born the vision for what would become the Make-A-Wish Foundation.

The first donation Make-A-Wish ever received was $15 from a grocery store manager. Frank Shankwitz was earning a few extra bucks working as a security guard at a grocery store, and that donation came from his manager after Frank told him about the plan to fulfill Chris Greicius's wish.

The Foundation received tax-exempt status in 1980, and by March 1981 had raised the $2,000 it needed to grant another very sick child's wish. A year later, eight wishes had been granted, all in the Phoenix area, when the Foundation was featured on *NBC Maga-*

zine. Linda Bergendahl-Pauling told the reporter what it meant to her son, and to her whole family, for Chris to have his dream come true before he died. Millions of viewers saw how their donations could touch the lives of a suffering child. In 2000, twenty years after Chris donned his police uniform, the Make-A-Wish Foundation granted its 80,000th wish.

The Make-A-Wish Foundation has been a very special part of our lives. As much as money is needed for research and how important it is to spend time with doctors and nurses and the people who make medicine for these kids, sometimes you just need a break from being your child's nurse and have time just to be a parent. When you spend a lot of time together, when you go through these life-threatening crises, when you live with a special need, sometimes it's critical to have a special time away together.

Megan and Patrick were Wish kids in 2001 and 2003, respectively. We went to Disney World both times—that's the most popular wish. Ever since, every time we ask the kids "Do you remember going to Disney?" they always say, "Oh heck, yeah, it was the greatest time! I remember going on this ride, and that event, and I remember you almost getting the handicap van towed." Apparently, you're not supposed to park in front of the flowers in the shape of Mickey's head, but some things in life you have to learn the hard way.

If you ask the kids today what special things they remember in life, they may talk about friends and family and school. Maybe they'll talk about the day they first got their enzyme therapy to help make them stronger. But they will always talk about their trips to Disney World. It's not just going to Disney World that's special. It was the opportunity both to feel special and at the same time to do something that a lot of kids get to do.

Several years after Patrick's trip, I asked Megan what she remembered about both visits. She recalled a startling amount from each, and we looked at some of the video and photos from the trip.

"You know, Dad, it's been a long time," Megan concluded.

"Yeah, Megan, it has been," I said. "You were about five years old for your trip and Patrick was seven for his."

It wasn't hard to guess what was coming. Pause. Finally, she spoke.

"When do we get to go on a Make-A-Wish trip again?"

"No, sweetie," I had to explain. "This is literally a once-in-a-lifetime special opportunity. The Foundation wants to make sure that every kid with a serious illness has a chance for a special trip, and that's why it's so special."

Megan seemed to understand. Until she finally said, "Aren't there any strings you can pull? You know people."

One of the many things about our family that Geeta Anand captures in her book about us, *The Cure*, is what those Make-A-Wish trips meant to us. She called the chapter "Making Memories," and that fits beautifully with the mission and vision of Make-A-Wish. These kids endure extraordinary tests in their young lives and show an amazing amount of strength. The ability to create memories beyond those challenges, happy and warm memories, instills in that child and his or her family a lifelong reminder of why life is so precious, the sense that there's a purpose to enduring those extraordinary tests. It reminds the child and family that life exists beyond a hospital room. The trip provides a chance to be a normal child and not just an eternal patient, a chance to live life and to share an experience with friends and family.

Creating these memories was the vision of Make-A-Wish, and that vision sustains the Foundation to this day, nearly 200,000 granted wishes later.

As it happens, somewhere around 60 percent of kids choose as their wish to go to Disney or on Disney cruises, which is great, and Disney is a huge supporter of the Foundation. But some of the other wishes—playing basketball with Michael Jordan, dog-sledding for a Florida boy who has never seen snow, spending a day with Harrison Ford on a movie set—create the kinds of memories that cannot be experienced any other way.

One teenager's dream was to accompany a *National Geographic* photographer on a shoot. He met the photographer in Vancouver, then joined him on a seaplane to a nearby island in the Canadian Pacific.

They photographed grizzlies, whales, and glaciers. When *National Geographic* published two of the boy's photos in its issue, he donated the money he received to fund the Foundation's trademark teddy bears for other sick children.

One preteen girl, a fan of the television show *Sex and the City*, made a wish to meet Kim Cattrall, who portrayed Samantha. This was not a typical wish for an inner-city kid, but Ms. Cattrall was up for it, so the Foundation put the pair together. What ended up happening shows how these wishes work both ways. Sure, it helps the sick child and her family. But it also helps those who make these wishes happen.

Ms. Cattrall and the young lady had lunch together. The average value of a wish is around $7,000, so usually with a celebrity meeting, there will also be personalized mementos, a hotel stay, and a gift. But these two hit it off, so instead of Ms. Cattrall simply handing over a box of autographed goodies and some presents, she said to the girl, "Do you have any plans tonight? I am supposed to attend a fancy awards show, and I don't have anyone to accompany me. Will you be my date?" The girl was stunned. And, of course, didn't have anything appropriate to wear.

Totally unplanned, Kim Cattrall took the girl shopping, bought her a necklace, got their hair done together, and took her to that awards show. She didn't seek publicity for it or put it on her Web site. She just humbly did a kind thing and gave a very sick little girl a thrill she will never forget.

Some kids have been more, shall we say, "creative" in their wish requests. My favorite request was from a seventeen-year-old boy struggling with leukemia. He had a wish to go to a party. In Beverly Hills. At a huge, luxurious mansion. A mansion owned by an elderly gentleman…named Hugh Hefner. Yes, he wanted to go to a party at Hef's mansion.(There's a reason there's no adult Make-A-Wish Foundation.)

As I understand it, the Board of the local Make-A-Wish chapter discussed this unique wish and concluded, despite many generous offers from Board members to provide adult chaperone services to the requested party, that it would not be possible to accommodate this particular wish. Good call. This young man and his family instead opted for an Alaskan cruise. Beautiful trip, we are told, with impressive vistas and peaks, although not quite the views he had in mind with his original request.

In the years that we have been involved with the Make-A-Wish Foundation, we have discovered that every kid invariably will describe the granted wish as a highlight of his or her life. As I write this, there are some forty very sick kids in America whose dream is to meet the Jonas Brothers. The Foundation doesn't just want to send them to a concert—that would be nice, but doesn't quite reach the level of "special" that Make-A-Wish prefers. Luckily, the Jonas Brothers heard about this, and said, "Let 's get it on the calendar in the next couple of months, because some of these kids don't have forever. Bring them all togeth-

er somewhere in the country for a private concert."
Each kid will get to bring their family and a friend.
What a lovely memory for these young children. And
that's the power of a vision that started with a little
boy in Arizona who wanted to be a policeman, just
for a day.

Incidentally, Megan wasn't thrilled when she heard
about the private concert, given our earlier conversation about the one-wish-per-kid limit. The Foundation
had an auction in New Jersey, at which Aileen and I
were honored for our past support. When the chance
to help grant a wish came up for bid, at $8,000, I put
up my hand and also raised John Jr.'s hand (he came
to the dinner with us to see us get the award). John Jr.
looked panicked as he whispered to me, "Dad, I don't
have $4,000!" I told him I'd cover his share. A few
weeks later a nice thank-you letter from the Foundation came, noting that our $8,000 donation had made
it possible for a young girl to go to a Jonas Brothers
concert and have a special visit with the brothers. How
nice. Megan took the letter from me and began reading. I sensed a lecture of sorts coming my way. With
a look of complete betrayal on her face, Megan said,
"Wait a minute. You paid for some other girl to go to
this concert, but not me? That is SO not fair." Moments like that remind me that for all of her preco-
ciousness, Megan is still a kid.

Make-A-Wish has been so successful and has had
such an impact on the lives of so many, because of its
simple but powerful vision. I believe that any organi-

zation needs to set a vision and work toward that vision with single-minded devotion. A great idea is only a beginning. One needs to envision a future before a plan to arrive at that destination can be crafted. One should be able to look out five, ten, twenty years or more and dream what something newly created can become—and then put a plan in place working backward for how to achieve that dream.

When your kids' lives are at stake, you have to take huge risks. But that doesn't mean reckless risks. Reckless risks consume time and other resources that must not be squandered. And they can set you back immensely in the quest toward your goal. So the idea is to set a vision, such as to develop a medicine to save your kids' lives, and formulate an ambitious yet realistic plan to accomplish that goal.

It's a value I have tried to instill in my own biotech company, Amicus Therapeutics. We don't have a mission statement, but instead use a "vision statement." It was developed by our employees, not our executives. It lets everyone—suppliers, partners, employees, customers, and investors—know exactly how we seek to run our company. Included in that vision statement are twenty-four ideals we strive for on a daily basis, including:

* We support the disease communities, and their families.
* We are passionate about what we do.
* We embrace constant innovation.

* We have a duty to obsolete our own technologies.
* We push ideas as far and as fast as possible.
* We take smart risks.
* We learn from our mistakes.
* Our medicines must be fairly priced and broadly accessible.
* We are business-led and science-driven.
* Diversity of experience and thought is essential.

These ideas didn't emerge from thin air. I left Genzyme in 2002, just weeks before Megan and Patrick began receiving their life-saving enzyme therapy. I was offered a number of business opportunities. Aileen likes to kid around that I retired for eleven weeks until she came home one day and found me reorganizing a couple of hundred photographs in chronological order. She insisted that I had to get out and get day work again.

Having built relationships with venture firms, I contacted some to see what was out there, and across my desk came a business plan from a company called Amicus. As a lawyer, I read that as a-MEE-kiss, as in the kind of briefs one files as a friend of the court, rather than AM-a-kiss (in either case, the word is Latin for "friend"). Regardless of pronunciation, after months of looking through business plans, and even helping to start a few other private biotech companies, this opportunity at Amicus was extremely interesting.

In discussing Pompe disease, as with many genetic diseases, I had always described it as Megan and Patrick "missing" an enzyme. They were lacking the enzyme that's supposed to break down sugar stored as glycogen. So the treatments we had developed were all focused on the idea of making a biologic medicine to replace that enzyme.

Well, it turns out Megan and Patrick are not missing the enzyme. They make just as much of the critical enzyme as anyone. They just don't make it right because of a single mutation in their DNA. Their bodies produce that one enzyme, but about 99 percent of it is discarded by the quality-control mechanisms in their cells, which have evolved to allow only perfectly made enzymes and proteins to do their jobs.

Amicus scientists thought, "Well, what if you had a drug that can interfere and bind to their own internally produced enzyme just as it's being made?" The binding could theoretically help the misfolded enzyme become more stable, and fold more properly, because proteins need to fold to work. Maybe then we could actually harness the power of their own naturally occurring enzyme and allow it to do what it needs to do, basically chaperoning it from one cell compartment to another (hence, the notion of a "friend"). Or perhaps the technology could potentially be used in some combination with the existing enzyme replacement therapies for these diseases, as with the one we helped develop for Pompe.

These were powerful ideas. Without turning this book into a molecular biology text, the point is that the more I learned about Amicus, the more excited I grew about the company. The problem was that they needed a new CEO. New Jersey's Economic Development Agency had opened up this incubator space to nurse along small technology businesses, and Amicus needed someone to take the business to the next level. After joining the company's Board in 2004, I agreed to become its CEO in January 2005—thanks to the powerful persuasion, and vision, of its board members Jamie Topper and Mike Raab.

The first thing I did at Amicus was lay out a vision that included many of the principles I've listed. We had about seven employees at the time. Two years later we went public in one of the larger biotechnology IPOs in 2007. Through all the twists and turns of running Amicus over the past several years, our vision statement has never changed. It has been the bedrock of our corporate values and a guiding force in our decision making. It represents what we must constantly aspire to achieve, and to be.

There is a lot of legitimacy to complaints about the pharmaceutical industry. But when you look at the overwhelming need for vision in the health care space and the tiny chance any one project has of bearing fruit in the world of drug development, the situation takes on a slightly different hue. In biotechnology, what you're selling is the future: You are selling data and hope. Small biotech companies don't have revenues.

They don't make products for sale. Their existence relies heavily on venture capital funding and eventually access to partnerships and public markets. These typically come forth in the hope that investors may recoup their money plus a sizable return when these companies hit key milestones, such as a drug showing strong clinical results or getting FDA approval for marketing.

Yes, if you get a drug approved, you can go from zero revenues to hundreds of millions within years, or even months. But that's *if* you get the drug approved, and it requires a massive commitment of time and money to make it through that process.

It's this extraordinary level of risk and investment to get a drug's approval, not the direct manufacturing costs, that drives the prices of medicines in the U.S. A biotech company can spend more than $800 million to develop just one new drug before it sees a dollar in revenue. And that's with an incredible lucky trajectory. If you're developing five drugs and one of them gets approved, then you've got to pay for those other four.

The pharmaceutical industry does a lot of things wrong in how it presents itself and markets its products. But things are getting better. They used to try to buy doctors with dinners and baseball games. And they still spend more on marketing than on R&D. But you know what? The computer software industry has better margins. Few complain about paying $200 for a copy of Microsoft Office, even though that particular copy costs less than a dollar to produce. It's understood that that one-dollar copy is the culmination of years and years of investment and hard work.

At its best, the American pharmaceutical industry represents the pinnacle of American vision and American dreaming. And the biotechnology industry is on the cutting edge of those dreams. As the nation struggles with health care and affordability of medicines, my deepest hope is that we realize that these industries can be a force for good, and that we remember the continued importance of making newer and better medicines. The greatest dream and vision is a world one day where words like "cancer" and "AIDS" are relegated to footnotes in medical textbooks. That's a big dream, that's a great vision, and that will happen—so long as we have the vision to keep chasing miracles like these.

Part III

JOY

Chapter 7

KEEP PERSPECTIVE

I had such a hard night with Patrick tonight. He wanted to look at himself in the full-length mirror. After about three minutes he began yelling, "Come on, move!" I asked him what was wrong and he said, "I can't move my arms. And my legs won't move, either." Patrick sat in front of that mirror for twenty minutes trying to move his arms and legs. I asked him if he was okay and he said, "I'm mad. I hate Pompe disease, and I want to be strong."

I tried to explain that his brain was strong and that he is a very special boy and that Mom and Dad are working very hard to get him stronger....yikes! This is the first time he has ever questioned anything. I took a long, hot shower crying my eyes out, then reached for a glass of wine...it's really been the first time I didn't have an answer for him.

Later on, I went into his room to roll him over and put him back to sleep. Again, he said, "Mom, I'm really sad that I can't move my arms and legs." Anyway, I just needed to vent....thanks for listening!

—An e-mail Aileen sent to five of her closest friends

The Crowley Fun Machine does not travel lightly. When people meet our family for the first time, they see tubes and ventilators, nurses and vans for the handicapped: controlled chaos in motion. Often, a look of pity will overtake them, and one can some-times detect a sense of relief of the "there but for the grace of God go I" variety.

The truth is, though, that ours is a joyful, warm home, and Aileen and I do our best to remind our-selves every day how blessed we are in so many ways. The e-mail that opens the chapter was one Aileen sent to her closest friends one autumn night in 2009. She purposefully didn't send it to me. I was traveling on business in California and it was a particularly stress-ful time for our company, so she didn't want to add an-other burden on me—another remarkable testament to Aileen's strength and resolve. I found out about this emotional message from one of my closest friends, whose wife had received it. I wasn't sure whom to feel worse for, Aileen or Patrick. But as quickly as this epi-sode occurred, it passed.

When I let Aileen know that I had read the e-mail, we embraced, talked for five minutes, cried, put it in perspective … and moved on. The only reason we could do so was because Patrick had shown us how. By the next morning, he was over his sadness, once again happy and talking about his karate class. We learn so much from our kids.

Both the heart-wrenching experience with Patrick that day and Aileen's need to vent to her friends are just so uncommon for us. Most days, we do what ev-ery family does: we try our best to enjoy each other's company and make the very most of the time we have together. The need to keep matters in their proper perspective is critical for all families. Special needs or not, all families have challenges. All families face a decision: Will we let the challenges defeat us or will we defeat the challenges? Our family has relied on two strategies to help us keep the perspective we need, not only to get through the day but to achieve the deeper balance and richer fulfillment that I associate with joy.

Humor

The first of these strategies is humor. We laugh—a lot. I've already described Megan's remarkable ability to feel empathy for other kids while not feeling sorry for herself. But Megan's also got a stinging wit, and she's not afraid to use it. Woe unto those unfortunate souls who are the targets of the princess's rapier sarcasm. I speak from experience, believe me. The most frequent target of Megan's wicked sense of humor is her big brother, John Jr. He's such a sweet and goofy kid that teasing him is shooting fish in a barrel for someone as sharp as Megan. It's like John Jr. is her unwitting Ed McMahon. But it's an important part of our family's dynamic and definitely helps maintain the perspective and balance we need.

When John Jr. turned fourteen, his longtime interest in computer games was evidently "supplemented" by an interest in other things that teenage boys may chance to look at on a computer. Once, Aileen discovered something inappropriate in the browsing history on our family computer. Of course, she blamed me. I fervently denied it. Really, it wasn't me. And she quickly removed me from the suspect list, largely because she figured I would have been smart enough to clear the history. So we approached John. He broke without even the threat of torture. We applied some good parenting: "It's healthy to be curious and you are very normal to want to look at naked ladies, but if you even think of looking at that Web site again, you *will* go blind *and* I *will* make you sleep in a box outside." Dr. Spock would be so proud.

John sheepishly apologized and felt genuinely remorseful. I asked him how he knew to go to *that* particular site. He said he Googled it. I asked: "Googled 'it'? What is 'it'?" He replied, even more sheepishly, "naked ladies." Quite frankly, if the Internet had been around when I was fourteen, that probably would have been my search strategy as well. I reiterated that he was to refrain from such digital adventures. We haven't had a problem since. We've found that passwords on the computers help ensure compliance as well. The episode passed and we moved on. We assumed that would be the end of it...until Megan let us know that she had overheard this little interchange with John.

A few days later, I heard John and Megan arguing over whose turn it was to use the computer. Apparently, John had been playing some Pokémon computer game when Megan zoomed in and tried to commandeer the computer. So I heard them yelling and arguing, which is in itself an interesting experience because to those who don't spend time with her, Megan's voice is very difficult to understand. She sounds kinda like Scooby-Doo.

Megan yelled, "You're not getting back on this computer!" and John yelled back, "Yes, I am!" So Megan says, "No, you're not. John. We all know that wicked, bad things happen when you go on the family Mac. I'm going to find an adult and kick you off that computer...porn king." Ouch, that one stung. I refereed a settlement—parenthood really is just an ongoing exercise in diplomacy. I don't know that all parents ought to view their bickering kids as a positive tool for maintaining perspective. But amid a decade of fretting for their very survival, it is kind of nice to hear them interact like normal kids arguing over computer time, trading barbs, and, of course, threatening blackmail.

As I look back on our lives together, Aileen and I have made it a point to find time to laugh even before we were facing the sorts of challenges that have played such a big role in our lives.

When I started at Harvard Business School, we moved to Cambridge in the middle of the winter. For a long time, the Harvard MBA program would allow part of each class to start in January, completing the first semester in the spring. Instead of doing an internship, you could do your second semester and then merge with the rest of the class to finish your next two semesters alongside the full class. You could do the whole four-semester MBA program in about seventeen months.

The students who started in January tended to be a bit older and have a bit more real-world experience, and that period represented the very first time I let my hair down a little bit. Well, the hair doesn't move much, so maybe not the most apt analogy, but you get the gist. I was raised with a profound sense of responsibility. Throughout all my years of schooling, I could feel the weight of my family's expectations—and my own. I pushed myself to the utmost of my capabilities in all that I did and was proud of the success I had achieved in academics and elsewhere.

Part of what drew me to Aileen was her sunny, easygoing attitude, so different from the competitive intensity I brought to all endeavors. Once I got into Harvard, I felt I could finally relax a little. The brass ring that an HBS education would ultimately provide—the education, the contacts, the prestige— would lay a foundation for us in life, one that no one in my family had ever enjoyed before. Quite frankly, I am still convinced that the HBS admission committee made a clerical error when they admitted me. I still have dreams that someone in the admissions office will realize this long-ago made mistake and seek to invalidate the degree.

The school itself represented the pinnacle of American academic achievement, and we had two happy little kids. The classwork was intense, but life was good. I finally felt I could relax in the way Aileen had always encouraged me to do. So I tried, and all the great friendships and camaraderie at HBS helped.

One story is a tad embarrassing, but provides a really nice example of the foundation underpinning our marriage and the ability to laugh at oneself.

Aileen is beloved by everyone she meets. Her warmth, easy smile, and infectious laugh put people instantly at ease—plus, she's absolutely gorgeous. And while I like to think I, too, have a good sense of humor and a decent amount of warmth, there's no denying that I have the more intense personality. As with the sons of a lot of cops and military men (I was both), there's a little bit of Boy Scout seriousness to my demeanor at times. Put it this way: If I had been a teenager during the late 1960s, I would not have been among those wearing bell-bottoms and long hair.

At Harvard, I would occasionally go out for drinks with my classmates, which I had very seldom done at Georgetown or Notre Dame. It was liberating to have a little fun after years of pouring myself into my studies and striving to be the best student I could be. Aileen loved and encouraged it. After all those years of earnestness and striving for perfection, I was finally cutting loose a little.

Now, it is my belief that certain details of the following story have been exaggerated as family legend has taken over from reality. But Aileen swears that on one occasion she was awakened late at night by a strange sound. I was standing in a corner of our small bedroom mumbling: "Aileen. Aileen. The light in the bathroom is out. And someone took the toilet." I had come home after having a beer or two too many. Apparently I had mistaken the corner of our bedroom for the bathroom. She flipped the light on which, as I recall, startled me greatly. She was even more startled to see me standing there about to pee, apparently not over-whelmingly concerned that a toilet thief had robbed us blind. She redirected me to the bathroom just in time. On the way back to bed, Aileen claims that I mumbled again as I settled in: "When did you add the new bath-room?" Legend, again, I firmly believe. Nonetheless, Aileen has laughed about this ever since and loves to tell the story whenever it will inflict maximum red-facedness, say, to other officers' wives at a gathering of Navy officers. Church dinners are another favorite.

I am still attributing this alleged incident to an undiagnosed bladder problem and delusions brought about by food poisoning; the Guinness played only a minor role. But the point of sharing this kind of story is to demonstrate how the marriage dynamic is an evolving, flexible being. With the challenges Aileen and I were about to face (Megan's diagnosis was a little more than a year away), we knew that we could change to adapt to different circumstances and never take ourselves too seriously.

When Megan hit the preteen years, she began to love the kind of chick flicks that a red-blooded American dad finds intolerable. One Saturday, I took John Jr. to South Bend for a Notre Dame game and didn't get him home and settled in until about midnight. I was ab-solutely zonked and took a long, hot shower before climbing into bed. Aileen was half sleeping while watching the ultimate chick flick, *Steel Magnolias*.

My testosterone-induced reflex to such a movie kicked in immediately and I registered an official protest requesting a channel change. Even the weather channel would be fine, but not this. While lying there, I recalled a funny incident that had happened a year earlier and when I reminded Aileen, we couldn't stop laughing.

In *Steel Magnolias*, there's a scene where Julia Roberts's character, the improbably named Shelby Eatenton Latcherie, goes into diabetic shock and convulses. Her mother, M'Lynn Eatenton, played by Sally Field, rushes out to try to get sugar into her system by pouring orange juice into her mouth. It's a serious scene and M'Lynn keeps repeating, "Oh Shelby, baby, come on, baby, stay with me, come on, take the orange juice, sweetie, stay there, stay there." I was watching the movie with Megan about a year earlier and she was tearing up at the drama, and no doubt relating it to her own experiences, and I said, "Megs, you don't have diabetes, too, do you?" She just shot me a withering glance, wondering what kind of caveman father would dare make light of a drama as stirring as *Steel Magnolias*.

Megan has always had a lighthearted and self-deprecating view of her Pompe disease. She has for years described it as a "minor breathing problem," always using air quotes when stating those words. She recently did concede some measure of lack of skeletal muscle strength, and now describes it as a "minor breathing *and* walking problem." Megan pities poor Shelby in the movie, despite the much more serious disease she endures every day of her life.

Anyway, about twenty minutes after we had watched that scene together last year, I couldn't take it anymore and went into the kitchen. All of a sudden Megan's vent starts beeping and she needs some suction. But it's slightly worse than usual; Megan is coughing and choking and her eyes are tearing. These respiratory episodes are the most frightening, and life-threatening, aspect of the disease that she and Patrick live with each day. I'm staying out of the way as Aileen handles it because there's no one better at this in the world. Megan looks over at me while Aileen's doing her hero-nurse-mom thing, and I can't resist.

"Oh, no, baby, Shelby baby," I start to wail, and I walk over to the fridge to grab a carton of Tropicana. "I can help, Shelby baby," I say, "just drink this orange juice." Megan is looking at me with this very shocked and annoyed stare, as if to say, "I can't believe what a creep I've got for a father" when all of a sudden she can't keep a straight face and she, too, begins laughing, while Aileen's still working on her. Aileen is the last of the three of us to give in to the irony of the moment, but when she does, she falls hard. Tears pour from all of our eyes.

I imagine that someone looking in on all this or reading this book would see that as pretty insensitive.

Maybe. But you've got to laugh, too. To this day, I will often come home from work and ask, "How's Shelby doing?" or if she's having a particularly bad breathing episode, one of us will hold her hand and say, "Come on, Shelby, baby" to calm her down and take her mind off what could otherwise be a terrifying episode.

Aileen has a knack for using humor to turn a tough or awkward situation into a positive one. Like a lot of Italian mothers in New Jersey, my mother always wanted me to marry the little Italian girl from Bergen County. Not that there was one in particular—there will never be a shortage of Italian girls in northern New Jersey—but that was my mother's unshakable image: the petite Italian girl with dark hair and big brown eyes from Norwood, maybe Northvale. So from day one, Aileen had to overcome the fact that she was not Italian. Worse, she was Irish, just like my father.

It's hardly uncommon for Italian girls to resent the attention Italian boys seem to shower on the red-haired, freckle-faced lasses who share the same schools, attend the same dances, and develop crushes of their own on Italian boys. As a matter of fact, that fictional drama about organized crime in northern New Jersey known as *The Sopranos* had a scene that perfectly captures this very dynamic. Jennifer Melfi, the psychiatrist played by Lorraine Bracco, is discussing with her ex-husband how they should spend the proceeds from a second home they've agreed to sell.

Dr. Melfi tells him, "Just don't spend it on one of your Colleens," referencing his interest in Irish women.

And speaking of Lorraine Bracco … I once saw her absolutely buck naked.

In 2002, Lorraine Bracco played Mrs. Robinson in a Broadway version of *The Graduate*. As Christmas presents, Aileen's cousin bought tickets for us and a couple of other cousins. We all went to the city together to make a night of it. Our seats happened to be in the very front row. Now, I had heard that Ms. Bracco appeared nude in the play, but I suppose to the degree I considered it, I imagined a dimly lit, veiled appearance for a fleeting moment. Um, no.

While Mrs. Robinson is working her magic on Benjamin Braddock, the next thing we know, Lorraine Bracco, four feet from us, drops her robe and stands absolutely naked above us but for a pair of high heels.

Afterward, all four couples went out for drinks. It was just a few days after Christmas, and this was our big night out without the kids. Aileen's brother Brian and his wife, Kim, were discussing their new baby. And the cousin who got us the tickets and her husband were discussing their kids. And I mentioned something about our kids. We were going to stay over that night in the city, and the whole point was to get away from the kids for a moment—it's no small matter to arrange all the sitters and nurses we need for a night out—yet here we were, all focused on the mundane minutiae of child rearing.

All of a sudden, Aileen piped up. "Enough! Guys, guys, guys—enough! Can we stop? We're young and we're out and here's a new rule: We're not talking about kids anymore." Everybody sort of looked around and nodded and said, "Yeah, you're right, Aileen. We're intelligent, engaged adults. Let's talk about something else." Silence. Nothing. Finally, someone sheepishly said, "Well, uh, what are we going to talk about?"

Exasperated, Aileen said, "You know what? Let's talk about Lorraine Bracco's private parts. Did anybody else see Lorraine Bracco's private parts?"

The whole table fell still. And then burst out laughing. To this day, if we're out and supposed to be having a date but instead allow the conversation to be dominated by the serious and consuming needs of our kids, Aileen will invoke the Lorraine Bracco Rule. And we'll remember to take an hour or two and speak to each other as adults who have a life beyond the special needs of our children. I am sure Ms. Bracco would love to know her nether regions have given their name to a rule that brought husband and wife closer together.

I believe it's critical for all parents, especially those of children whose special needs rightfully command extra attention, to maintain a relationship independent of the children. Not just for the sanity of the husband and wife. Actually, it's the kids who benefit the most. Nothing goes farther toward creating happy, confident children than parents who are happy together. Especially in the case of children with special needs, the children greatly benefit from the knowledge that the

added burdens of providing for their care have not ru-
ined the family or sapped its energy. There's no better
way for parents to send that message to a child than by
simply enjoying each other's company.

Humility

The other strategy we use to maintain perspective, to
remind ourselves how blessed we are, is humility.

During my first year of law school, I was feeling a
little sorry for myself. The old saw about working first
years to death definitely applied at Notre Dame. I was
suffering the drudgery of a South Bend winter, while
Aileen was finishing her senior year of college and living it up.

One of the things that helped me was the sense of
faith that pervaded the university. If you didn't want to
participate, you didn't have to, particularly as a graduate or a law student. But it was such an important part
of campus life and the character of the university. It is
difficult for even the most casual Catholic not to be
moved by the statue of the Blessed Virgin Mary at the
Grotto of Our Lady of Lourdes. It's a special place and
it's also a place where you find faith.

Notre Dame is also a place where one can feel
humbled, tiny against the enormousness of human
history and God's handiwork.

In the fall of 1991, some six or seven months after
the first Gulf War ended, Aileen and I went to a Notre
Dame football game, which I attended as often as I
could. At every Irish game, they honor somebody at

halftime, and I was half paying attention when they brought out this woman and her young children. Her husband had attended Notre Dame. He was an army pilot and he died in the war.

It was a beautiful, sunny fall day and the widow began by thanking the university administrators for the beautiful plaque she'd been given to honor her husband's memory. What she said next snapped my mind from wandering and suddenly I was paying rapt attention. This young woman's words touched me deeply, and reflected the spirit of Notre Dame in a more personal way than I had ever experienced before or have experienced since. Recalling those words from nearly twenty years ago as best as I can, she said: "God, I wish my husband were here with us now. This would have been the perfect day for him, because everything that he cared most deeply about in life is here today." The young widow paused and pointed at the stadium and the "Touchdown Jesus" mural on the Hesburgh Library and then she listed those things. She pointed at the mural and said, "His God," then she pointed at her two little kids and said, "his family," then she looked over at the ROTC Honor Guard that was on the field and she said, "his country," then she gestured toward the entire crowd and said, "and his Fighting Irish." These were the things that mattered to this fellow, a man who died defending his fellow Americans, people he would never meet, including everyone in the stadium that day.

I thought about my dad, and how one of the very last memories I have of him is teaching me to love

Notre Dame football. When you grow up in a family where no one went to college, there's a very good chance your Irish Catholic father will select Notre Dame as your team. The first time I saw the Notre Dame football team play on television was January 1, 1975. I was seven years old. My dad had regaled me with stories of the legends of Irish football, and on that chilly January night, we were ready to watch our first Notre Dame game together as father and son. I remember being mesmerized by the glow of the stadium lights off the golden helmets. Notre Dame edged Alabama in that Orange Bowl, 13 to 11. I was forever hooked on ND football.

After the game, I asked my dad for a helmet just like the ones the Notre Dame players wore. The next day, he took me to Sears. We bought a generic white football helmet and together we spray-painted it gold. Twelve days later my dad, my hero, died. I held on to that helmet. I still have it today, and I never forgot what it felt like to sit on the couch next to my dad, cheering on the Irish.

Aileen and I spoke later that night about how moving the widow's presentation at the Notre Dame game had been. It brought back these memories of my father, and I realized that seeing her determination and strength and hearing about her husband's sacrifice had affected me very deeply. These few things gave purpose to his life and probably comprised the foundation of whatever level of faith he may have had. I believe that's very important, no matter what one does—

whether you're a blue-collar laborer or the President of the United States. Always remember the bigger purpose and feel good about playing even a small role in a worthy, larger enterprise. It is humbling, indeed.

I don't mean to suggest that it's easy to maintain proper perspective at all times. It ain't. No one is immune to the little irritants in life. My law school roommate, Dave Gorman, has remained a good friend over the years. His dad had been a real salt of the earth, pulled up by the bootstraps, Irish Catholic guy who had built a successful business and managed to send his son to Notre Dame Law. I remember being out to dinner with them in the South Bend years, and David and I were complaining about law school and the workload and "it isn't fair" and "the weather is awful." Mr. Gorman just listened to us and nodded and finally laughed and said, "You know what, guys? You have no idea of the challenges that are ahead of you in life. Your happiness is going to be directly proportional to how you handle those challenges." Sage advice from a good man.

Humility is particularly important when a string of good news starts to make you feel just a little big for your breeches. Luckily for me, no one is better at bringing someone down to earth than my daughter, Megan.

By the time I became CEO of Amicus, I had learned a thing or two about running a business. For all the mistakes I made at the earlier biotech businesses I had run, companies that were ultimately successful, at Amicus I actually kind of knew what I was doing. The company was growing, and by May 2007 we were preparing for an initial public offering. We went on a "road show" and were being represented by the biggest and best investment banks in the world. The road show before a highly anticipated IPO is an incredible experience. After years of struggle, suddenly the most prestigious investors in the world are clamoring to offer you money. Our bankers gave us a Gulfstream jet to travel around the country to meet these accounts, and we had our choice of investors. Amicus ended up doing one of the most successful biotech IPO in years in terms of valuation. The market value of the company, worth $8 million just two and a half years earlier, was suddenly $300 million.

On the night before the IPO, the bank provided this great big suite at the Palace Hotel. I hadn't seen Aileen in two weeks because we were on the road show and she came into the city to spend the night. We were scheduled to ring the closing bell at Nasdaq the next day, our first day of trading. I told my head of human resources, "You know what? We're going to celebrate." We had maybe seventy-five people in the company at that time, and I invited everybody and a guest to come to the city to celebrate the festivities as a company.

We started the morning opening the stock on the floor at Morgan Stanley's trading operation. We were in the *Wall Street Journal* and then had lunch at Tavern on the Green. We had a ludicrously large limo taking us around the city. We were thrilled that we were going to have the money to pursue revolutionary cures, and meanwhile we had made a lot of good, hard-working people at the company pretty rich. When you close the Nasdaq stock exchange, you write your signature on a Lucite board and press a buzzer to close the whole stock exchange, and it's shown live on TV, as well as on this great big video screen outside of Nasdaq's Times Square headquarters. They broadcast my signature, my photo, and the Amicus logo for twenty minutes live in Times Square. With my entire team around me and the relief of having pulled off a successful IPO, I felt pretty good about myself professionally.

Aileen and I didn't stay at the party very long. I was exhausted after those couple of weeks and we went home. When we walked in, Aileen went upstairs and came down to report, "Megan is still awake, she wants to see you." I wore a yellow power tie and white shirt and blue suit and was feeling very CEOish when I walked in to see her. I said, "Hi, Megan, Daddy missed you." She replied, "I missed you so much, Daddy." She threw her arms open, inviting me in for a warm embrace. Then she told me that her friends had all been over in the afternoon when Mommy called to tell them to turn the TV on to CNBC. She said, "I saw you on TV today!" I replied quite self-assuredly, "Yeah, Megs, Daddy did pretty good this week. So how did the old man look on TV?" She looked me in the eye and said, "Well, honestly, you looked really, really, really"—I assumed she was going to say "handsome" or "powerful"—"really, really . . . short."

I am not a tall man. As it happens, the fellow on my right was about 6'5" and the one on my left was 6'4" and I was on TV sandwiched between these two giants and the podium was up to my neck. It did make me look extra short.

So I just looked at her and this great big sense of accomplishment was deflated in an instant by my little girl whose only thought was, "Gosh, my dad sure is . . . short." She realized what she had said, and she tried to save it by saying, "Oh, but it's okay. I really like your tie." I laughed and hugged her and said, "Thanks, Meg. Thanks."

She said, "You're welcome. I love you!" and gave me a kiss and went to sleep with this big smile on her face. I thought of all the wonderful professional accomplishments that had culminated in the road show and IPO and then I looked at my beautiful little girl, her ventilator quietly humming as it filled her broken lungs. How blessed it is to have children, who love you for reading them stories and putting them to sleep, not for IPOs and snazzy road shows.

One Sunday after we returned from Portland, where the movie about us was shot, we had a particularly trying day. Aileen was about to make dinner and said, "You know what? The hell with it—we're going out." The studio had sent the family a bunch of baseball caps that they had made for the cast and crew. They're very official-looking, very Hollywood, with a black crown and "Crowley" across the front with a

Nike swoosh, and "CBS Films * Portland 2009" on the side. All five of us put on the hats, piled into the vans, and off we went to Friendly's. There was a time not so long ago when I would have been self-conscious to be sitting there with the wheelchairs and the vents in a crowded restaurant wearing matching hats with our name on it. Not anymore. Instead, I focus on how lucky I am to have my family around me. They are what it's all about. They are the center of the "it" when I remember that "it" is bigger than me.

CHAPTER 8

OUR MORTALITY MAKES US SPECIAL

> *Knowledge of our own mortality is the great-*
> *est gift God ever gives us because unless you*
> *know the clock is ticking, it is so easy to*
> *waste our days, our lives.—Anna Quindlen*

I've talked quite a bit with others who have lost a parent at an early age. It's common for those who have suffered a traumatic loss to fear death to a greater degree than most, and to fantasize about living forever. Despite the medical miracles I see on a daily basis, and my increasing conviction that it will soon be possible to live a very, very long time, I wouldn't choose to live forever. I think it's our mortality that makes us special and makes us appreciate every day. Our mortality makes us act in ways that enhance life and elevate our souls.

In November 2007, we came very close to losing Megan yet again. Aileen called me at work and I said, "Hey, hon, I'm busy, what's up?" Aileen said, "Oh, nothing." "Can I call you later?" I asked. Aileen replied, "Well, it's just . . . Megan had an incident at school." I asked, "What happened?" Aileen suddenly started bawling and said, "She had a plug, and we almost lost her."

This had happened once before. It's different from the manual suction she needs a few times a day to clear the mucus and saliva from her upper airways. What Aileen refers to as a "plug" is when Megan's bronchial tube is capped and it's as if somebody grabbed her throat and completely cut off her air supply. Picture a cork shoved down your throat, but even deeper—right where the bronchial tubes branch into the lungs.

Megan was in class at the time and her nurse, Sharon, was there. Sharon has worked with us since 1999 and has been an instrumental part of the kids' lives and of ours. With her booming voice and Arkansas accent, she is an unlikely but complete member of the Crowley family.

Megan was working on a project with a friend when suddenly she couldn't breathe. She looked at Sharon and pointed to her throat to say, "I can't breathe." Sharon suctioned Megs immediately, but nothing came up. She frantically changed Megan's trachea tube, but that didn't help, either. Megan began turning blue. Then she passed out. And that's when the teacher gathered all the children and ran out of the classroom.

She wanted Sharon to do what she needed to do and also, I'm sure, didn't want to be in the room with the kids if Megan died, as was looking increasingly likely during those perilous few minutes. Sharon pulled Megan out of her chair and began emergency measures to save her life. Sharon just kept forcing air in, forcing saline water down the trachea, until the plug finally dislodged and Sharon was able to clear the airway and bring Megan back.

Even as Aileen told me the story, I was walking out the door at work, racing home. Forty minutes later, I walked in the house and saw Sharon, her eyes still puffy from crying over the ordeal. I hugged her and she started crying again, and said, "Oh, John, you just never know...." I said, simply, "Thank you." And I walked into Megan's bedroom.

Megan was in bed watching TV. I said, "Sweetie, are you okay?" She replied somewhat softly, "Yeah, I'm fine now." I said, "I know you were scared." She said, "Yeah, it was pretty scary, Dad." I looked at her and I said, "Sweetie, you are the bravest little person in the world."

I struggled to hold my emotions in check as I asked her, "Is there anything I can do for you, Megs?" Patrick had been very sick in the hospital about three weeks earlier, and we had just gotten him this big plasma TV for his room to welcome him back. Megan eyeballed the dinky thirteen-inch in her room and pointed to it with a look of utter disgust. She said, "Well, Dad, there is one thing... Can I have a great big plasma TV like Patrick's?"

I just looked at her and I said, "Absolutely." I stroked her hair a little bit and then walked out. It occurred to me as I left my daughter's room that if I had nearly died an hour or so earlier, I probably wouldn't have thought to use that as leverage to secure a new television. Even in the face of her own mortality, she had the good sense to know how to play me like a fiddle. Well played, Megs.

I have spent a decade committed to the idea of extending and improving human life through the advancement of science and medicine. I have seen miracles and believe that today's scientific technologies have us on the edge of a golden age of medicine. I truly think that within twenty years, many of humanity's most-feared diseases will be eradicated or no longer deadly: most cancers, multiple sclerosis, Parkinson's disease, Alzheimer's, cystic fibrosis. Many now-fatal disorders will be diagnosed readily and treated with a cocktail of different drugs, much like the paradigm that has evolved for the treatment of AIDS. Having watched my own children and countless others suffer through debilitating, painful, awful diseases, I look forward to that day with great anticipation. At the same time, there is something very special about making the most of every day one has here and now. Raising two children who have been very close to death several times has taught Aileen and me to savor every moment. The mundane activities and even the difficult spells—all of them are gifts from God, chances to be in the same place at the same time with our very special children.

When we first started to get our hands around Pompe disease and how deadly it was, we kind of set a stake in the ground—the one and only time we ever did that. We thought to ourselves, and even prayed,

"Just let our little girl get to two years old." She was fifteen months at the time and newly diagnosed.

When Megan survived that series of life-threatening illnesses and complications from Pompe in the fall of 1998, a miracle had taken place. As parents, when you get to that stage where you're preparing for the death of a child and are given the gift of a miracle, you experience a renewed sense of commitment and faith. After those six weeks in the intensive care unit, we never again thought about whether Megan would live to a specific age. As we started to discover that there were scientists and doctors working on this and that there actually was a little bit of hope, we stopped thinking like that. We just tried to focus on keeping Megan and Patrick as long as we can, and we never again defined what "long" was.

It may be a cliché to note that every day is a gift, but given the precariousness of our children's lives, we've come to appreciate that gift on a particularly forceful and vivid level. It shouldn't take near-death experiences to win that sense of wonder over the moments we're given to enjoy life. By the time the kids had gotten sick, I had already had plenty of moments, including my father's sudden death when I was a child, that should have imbued in me a sense of how precious life could be. Still, it took those dark days in the hospital in the fall of 1998 to take the meaning of that cliché to heart.

About a month after Megan's respiratory episode at school in 2007, she and I were Christmas shopping in downtown Princeton. As we were driving home, her ventilator beeped and we had to pull over. She needed a routine suctioning, and as I probed the tubes down her throat, I kidded with her and said, "Megs, don't throw up a lung like you did with Sharon last month. I'm not prepared for that." Megan replied, "I'm fine, it's no big deal." I said, "I know, honey."

We started driving home and I caught a glimpse in the rearview mirror of my strong, brilliant, beautiful daughter. I told her, "You know, Megan, we always save you. I know it's scary and once or twice you've blacked out. But you have the best people around you, and we love you and always take care of you." Megan simply replied, "Yeah, I know." I tried again. I knew where I wanted to go and the point I wanted to make, but struggled to put it into words. I said, "Honey, someday we're all going to die. When you do die, it will be a long, long time from now. But if you ever do think you're going to die, don't be afraid. It's not something to fear. When you go to heaven, you'll have eternity and be in heaven with all the people you love and when you get there, all the people who have gone before you will be there to meet you so that you're not scared."

I felt somebody should share that perspective with her. Based on her experience, character, and intellect, few eleven-year-olds have Megan's capacity to appreciate this type of reflection. I asked her, "Honey, when you get to Heaven, who do you think will be the first person to meet you after Jesus?" I was thinking she'd talk about my dad, my grandfather, her Aunt Mary. She thought about the question a good long while. Finally, she looked in the mirror and caught my eyes and said matter-of-factly, "I don't know. You, I guess." A giant smile formed on my face, even as tears began to fill my eyes.

Part of appreciating the specialness of mortality is learning to put minor slights behind you. Life is far too short to allow distance to creep into the space between yourself and the people you love.

I learned that lesson from an early age.

My dad's brother Jimmy had been very close to our family, and we saw him constantly when I was young. He is as loving and full of life an Irishman as you'll ever meet. His kids were more like siblings to us than cousins. For years when I was younger, we all lived in the same garden apartment complex. When my dad died, Uncle Jimmy was understandably devastated by the loss of his older brother. He was only thirty-two and suffered greatly with the weight of losing his best friend, his big brother. Some of that pain was expressed as anger toward my mother.

All of a sudden, Uncle Jimmy was essentially out of our lives. It was a jarring loss, coming so soon after losing my dad. A few years later, when I was twelve, we were having Sunday dinner at a diner, just my mother, my brother Joe, and myself. A young girl walked by and I said, "Mom, I think that's cousin Laura." It was the oddest thing. We had gone from seeing her every single day to never seeing her, and it wasn't as though they had moved to Hong Kong. There was enough turmoil in our lives that I never questioned exactly what had happened.

My mom said, "Yes, it is." Then I looked over to where Laura was sitting and I said, "Hey, that's Uncle Jimmy and Aunt Marie." We had seen Uncle Jimmy only a few times since my dad had died. Joe and I were beside ourselves to see our cousins. I told Mom, "This is great! We found them!" We walked over to their table and sat down and just started talking. Finally, my mother came over, too. I imagine it was awkward for her and for Uncle Jimmy. But it was time to bury the hatchet. We started seeing them again and quickly rediscovered the warmth that had been missing during those years when we didn't speak. We are now as close as any cousins can be, and Uncle Jimmy is like a second father to me today.

Our mother was heroic in raising us as a widow, not just working the late shift as a waitress but also instilling in us the importance of education and behaving respectfully.

We tell our son John constantly that all kids are different. As a youngster, my brother Joe was more emotional than most and he struggled. In retrospect, he would probably be diagnosed with ADHD and put on Ritalin today, but that wasn't done in those days. It hurt him in school and in some social relationships. And he never completely healed from our dad's death.

Joe is a very bright guy, but he always labored to find his way. I would sit in my room and read Bobby Kennedy's speeches and look at the globe and wonder about visiting places all over the world—pretty geeky stuff. Joe wasn't like that. He needed constant action. Joe and I used to fight all the time but we were also incredibly close, in a way that will be familiar to other kids who grew up without one of their parents.

Through it all, we've managed to stay great friends. He's always had a special place in his heart for our kids. And because he's lived at our house from time to time, they've gotten a real chance to know him. Still, it has been a bumpy ride for Joe.

Following in our dad's footsteps, Joe became a cop, eventually joining the force in Baltimore. He spent about ten years in uniform, but eventually he moved on to a series of business jobs.

My brother and I have taken very different paths. But we've managed to stay remarkably close. Sure, I put him in timeout and don't talk to him for weeks on end at times, but we still stay close. Losing our father at such a young age taught us early on to treasure whatever time we're given with those we love. And after the kids were diagnosed, Aileen and I have learned to accept imperfections not just in the kids but in all our loved ones, and in ourselves, and even welcome them as reminders that people are different and thank God for that. Joe's got a heart of gold and brings a specialness to our lives. He's part of the fabric of us.

The Quality of Life

As we began to get our heads around what it would mean to raise two children with very precarious health, Aileen and I developed a philosophy. We decided we would emphasize quality of life over quantity of life.

From the very beginning, Aileen and I instinctively agreed that we would prefer to make the kids as comfortable and happy as we could at home whenever possible, rather than subjecting them to hospitals and doctors' offices. Naturally, there will arise different opinions about when a prospective treatment is worth the discomfort. We've had different intensities and sometimes I've pushed harder or Aileen has pushed harder. But generally, without ever really discussing it or analyzing it, we have reached the conclusion that the kids are better off at home and that there's not a hospital nurse or doctor in the world who can administer to their day-to-day needs as well as the two of us and our best home nurses can.

When Patrick was sick in the hospital in the fall of 2007, he developed an ear infection that spread to the mastoid part of his temporal bone. The doctors wanted to try all these treatments and drugs and observe him for days, if not weeks. It was awful and he was in such pain, and stayed in the hospital for a couple of days and received antibiotics that saved his life. He was just so miserable and we were taking turns sleeping with him. The doctor thought it might be worthwhile to try a surgical procedure. We looked at our son and said to each other, "My God,

186

is this the right thing? Is he happy? Is he in pain? Is he suffering?"

Aileen didn't hesitate. She decided to bring him home.

The doctors tried to argue with us, accusing us of being completely naïve or uncaring or both. They insisted that he was sick and needed to try every possible remedy, no matter how little chance for success or how much additional suffering it caused. We actually ended up in a heated argument with the doctor, who came close to accusing us of abusing our son.

That's been the tougher part to balance. Whereas Aileen and I have always been on the same page, it's occasionally tougher to stand up to the pressure exerted by others who have an interest: doctors, nurses, teachers, even other family members. But our feeling has been that we want the kids to be as comfortable and happy as possible, surrounded by the people who love them most.

We actually had a nurse quit on us over the same kind of issue. On Christmas Eve 2008, Megan began to feel very sick. On Christmas morning, she was really dragging. I went to get her and said, "Come on, Megs, let's go down and open presents." Usually, Megan is knocking stuff over to get down to the tree and <u>tear open her gifts</u>.* She just wasn't herself, and an

---

*Megan has very strong opinions about Christmas. I wish I could claim they were based entirely on the sanctity of the birth of our religion's savior, but I'm afraid there's something more to it than that. One time, Megan and I were discussing religion with Dr. Slonim, who also happens to be

hour later went right back up to bed. It's always tough around Christmas because our key nurse, Sharon, is gone for the holidays for a much-needed break, and the nursing schedule is light.

Megan just got sicker and sicker. This had happened once before, when a simple flu grew into something much more serious. When Megan gets a lot of secretions in her chest or a bad chest infection, she can't cough it up like a regular kid can. With her added breathing difficulties, it gets to the point where she requires suctioning every two to three minutes to prevent being strangled by the secretions. Unfortunately, all that suctioning causes trauma to the trachea, which

an Orthodox Jew, and Megan was grilling him about Jewish traditions and rituals. She seemed pretty interested until Dr. Slonim mentioned that Hanukkah was wonderful because kids receive a present each night for eight nights. Megan did the math, and that pretty much ended her interest in Judaism. She told Dr. Slonim that she did way better than eight presents on Christmas and could not imagine getting by on any fewer.

Megan is deeply spiritual and prays with great intensity. But she stopped believing in Santa when she was five. She understands that the gift part of Christmas is a family's way of celebrating a holy day. John Jr., on the other hand, is fourteen and still believes in Santa Claus. Not so much as a jolly guy in a red suit, but more as a form of the Holy Ghost. Megan accuses John Jr. of still believing in the Easter Bunny. I'm not sure that's accurate, but it really is a sweet and innocent part of John's personality. His younger cousins will kid him and say, "You really believe in Santa Claus?" And he'll answer matter-of-fact, "Yes, I do."

starts to bruise and then bleed. The suctioning then begins to pull up bloody secretions, and it's hard to judge whether the suctioning itself is actually making it harder to breathe.

For three days we were suctioning up bloody mucus, and finally the night nurse came to Aileen and me and said, "I disagree with what you're doing. Megan needs to be in an emergency room in a hospital." Aileen replied, "There is nothing they can do for her in the hospital that we can't do here. It's that simple."

The nurse said, "She needs an X ray." Aileen shot back, "She doesn't need an X ray. All the X ray will show is that she has pneumonia, and we know that."

The nurse was afraid of losing her license if something happened on her watch. She took very good care of the kids and was a wonderful nurse, but she got spooked and decided she couldn't work with us anymore.

Left unsaid was the fact that Aileen and I had been forced to consider these issues many times. We can do just about everything for them in the house that can be done in a hospital. I'm not referring to chicken soup and a hot bath. Our home is equipped to provide excellent palliative care, but also to handle a variety of situations likely to arise for kids like Megan and Patrick. In essence, we have a miniature pediatric intensive care unit right in our home.

With the reduced nursing schedule during that holiday season, there was little we could do but take turns lying in bed with Megan, rubbing her head and giving her massages.

Eventually, Megan turned the corner and started to feel better. The simple fact is that if you show up in an emergency room with a kid who has a disease most doctors have never heard of, and is in a wheelchair and on a ventilator, honestly, they don't know what the hell to do with her. One can only guess who the heck is on duty in an emergency room at Christmas. And at least the kids are not going to pick up a staph infection at home.

The truth is, if the worst ever came, we don't want the kids to be in a hospital with twenty doctors and nurses standing over them and Code Blues buzzing. That's part of the balance I'm getting at when I describe wanting to emphasize quality of life.

These are questions that all parents of sick kids face. There are a lot of Pompe parents who make the very difficult and personal decision not to put their kids on a ventilator. They feel that the inability to breathe on one's own, along with all the other challenges a Pompe kid faces, leaves not enough pleasure left to make life worth living. There are other families who make a choice in the other direction. They never let their children leave the house and force visitors to put on sterile gowns, lest the kids catch an infection that could kill them. Each family has to find its balance. And that applies to all families, not just those whose kids have life-threatening diseases.

Had we put Megan in the hospital that Christmas, might there have been some statistical survival advantage? Maybe if her heart stopped, they would have equipment and expertise to restart it that wasn't available at our house. But that's part of the tradeoff. There is a balance to just how far you will go to intercede, to cause pain, to cause discomfort beyond the extraordinary measures that have already been taken. There is value to living life day to day as a person who can occasionally forget she has a dread disease, versus the goal of merely surviving for as long as possible.

We are fortunate to be able to supply the best nursing care and the best medicines available. But honestly, even this decision is one of balance. If somebody could guarantee that our kids would live another twenty years if we kept them in isolation, maybe we would. Maybe we'd skip the birthday parties and vacations and Jonas Brothers concerts. But we don't have any real reason to believe that. And we do take precautions, so there are accommodations to the fact that they're simply more vulnerable than healthy kids. If there's a flu outbreak at school, they don't go. We wash our hands more than any family on earth, and Sharon inoculates everyone who walks in the house with the annual flu vaccine.

Patrick also refuses to let life slip by. When it was time for him to start first grade, we struggled in deciding whether he should join Megan at regular public school. Patrick is physically weaker than Megan, and he's also a quieter kid. He has a tougher time integrating, and kids sometimes have difficulty relating to Patrick since he's not as bold and charismatic as Megan. Even going into kindergarten, I thought he should be home-schooled. It would have been logistically easier for us, and I thought he might enjoy it better. Aileen was adamant that he should attend regular school. We had some very intense discussions about it, and Aileen's viewpoint prevailed, as it should have. Patrick would not be half the person he is today had he not experienced public school over the past six years. He loves his teachers, he loves his classes, and he loves his friends. Last summer, he wanted to join the Princeton Police Academy program for youth. Five years earlier, I would have fretted about how embarrassing and difficult that would be. Having seen him succeed in school, we signed him up. He loved it, and the Princeton Township police loved him. He still wears today the Princeton Township pin on his hat that he received at graduation from the Youth Academy. He tells me he wants to be a policeman when he grows up "like my grandpa John." His character and strength have given me character and strength.

Someone once asked us if we ever regret the decision to put our kids on ventilators. After a horrible experience like Megan's that Christmas, do we ever wonder if maybe we had extended our kids' lives in a way that was unendurably difficult for them? The truth is, neither of us has ever regretted it, not during their worst health episode. If it ever even crosses our mind, the answer is simple. We look at our kids. They have great lives. And they enhance our lives and the lives of everybody they meet. That was true before there were movies and books about their lives, and even more so as those who will never meet these special children find themselves inspired by their strength and determination. As D. H. Lawrence once said: "Life is meant to be spent, not saved." And the Crowleys have spent a lot of life.

CHAPTER 9

THE BEARABLE UNIQUENESS OF BEING

Holleran family reunion, summer 2009, Scranton, Pennsylvania.

Many of Aileen's family have not seen Megan or Patrick in years. Aileen's older aunts and cousins— there are many—are lovely and have a sweet way of speaking to everyone as though they're five years old. Especially, it would appear, kids who are in wheelchairs and on ventilators. One particularly well-intentioned aunt comes over to greet the kids and her eyes grow very wide as she slowly says, "Oh, my goodness, these must be the children! I haven't laid eyes on you for ages!" She continues to make an elaborate fuss, addressing Megan and Patrick with a very sweet, sing-song patter. Finally, Megan leans over to Aileen. In what passes for a stage whisper for someone on a ventilator, she says to her mother, "Does she know I'm not stupid?"

After that terrible Christmas week when Megan came down with pneumonia, Aileen and I were exhausted from trading shifts all night with Megan, plus caring for Patrick. We were relieved to have a couple of quiet days finally. For a Christmas present,

I (actually, "Santa") had bought Megan a board game called Genetics. It laid out in a fun way the basics of inheritance—Mendel and fruit flies and all that. Board games for geeks...I have clearly been hanging out with Ph.D.s way too long.

I gave her a simple example as we started playing. Let's say, I explained, that I have brown eyes but my dad has blue, then I have a recessive gene, since someone with blue eyes has two recessive genes and will thus always contribute one to his offspring. Two parents who each carry one gene for brown eyes and one for blue will have a 25 percent chance of having a blue-eyed child: BB, Bb, bB, or bb.

She grasped it right away. After we went through a couple more examples, I said to Megan, "Now, do you know how you have Pompe?"

"Well, I assume I got it from Mom," she replied.

"Why would you think that?" I asked.

"Well, she gave birth to me, not you," Megan said.

I laughed and told her, "I know, honey, but 50 percent of you is from me and 50 percent from Mom."

I redid the cards, and instead of brown/blue we arranged them as Pompe/no Pompe. We looked at how, given that I'm a carrier and Aileen's a carrier, there was a 1 in 4 chance that any child of ours would have Pompe and a 1 in 4 chance that a child of ours would not have Pompe but be a carrier. Just then Aileen had woken up from a nap and was coming down the stairs. "What are you guys doing?" she asked, and I told her we were playing the Genetics board game. Aileen sarcastically observed, "Oh, *that* sounds like fun." Megan protested, "No, Mom, it's the coolest game. Guess what I learned? My Pompe—it's not *all* your fault. It's Dad's fault, too. I had no idea!"

Aileen looked at her incredulously. Finally, she said, "Megan, this whole time, you seriously thought this was all my fault?" Megan replied sheepishly, "I don't know, I figured I got it somehow when I came out of you."

That one episode represents the most we've ever discussed Pompe disease with the kids, at least the genetic basis for their disorder. My bright, curious children simply aren't all that interested in the one fact of their lives that is naturally of immense interest to anyone who meets them.

Earlier in this book I discussed the importance of diversity, how critical it is to trust in the ability of others to see our differences as a wonderfully enriching element of humanity. Here I'm talking about something different. When I refer to the "bearable uniqueness of being," I'm trying to convey a feeling not about how others view those with particular challenges. It's more about how those with challenges view themselves. It's about developing the spirit and strength to look at the challenges life throws your way and see them as integral parts of who you are and who you were intended to become.

When *Extraordinary Measures* was being filmed, one of the scenes we watched was Keri Russell, who plays Aileen, loading the kids into the handicapped van. Like much of what's in the movie, the details were eerily true to our actual lives. The house looked very similar to our house, their costumes were replicas of our clothes, and the wheelchairs and van were the same models as our family's. Something Aileen and I accomplish on a daily basis without a second thought really does look like an ordeal when acted out by others. We watched that one scene being filmed over and over for four hours, and it was very strange for the kids to see in such stark relief how difficult it can be simply to get moving in the morning.

The set of a major motion picture is mind-boggling. There are hundreds of people swarming in and out of dozens of trailers. It resembles a military operation. Aileen and I visited the set several times over the two months of filming and just couldn't get over all this machinery and human capital being deployed to tell our story, not to mention all the money invested in this project. At one point, I looked at Aileen and said, "All this because you forgot to take your birth control pills." She shot back, "Yes, all this because *you* had to get laid during a 'break' from the St. Patrick's Day Parade in New York in 1996." (Suffice it to say that green beer on March 17 is a wonderful aphrodisiac, at least for my Irish wife.)

Having Pompe disease makes it uncommon for Megan and Patrick ever to forget that they're different from other kids. But John Jr. is very different as well, and in some ways his challenges are just as great.

John Jr. was a late walker, not taking his first step until nineteen months. He was also a very late talker; his first word, "buddy," came at three years old. When he was months old, he would sit in his car seat and kick like crazy the entire ride, as if he were in an aerobics class.

As a baby, he simply could not sit still to eat a meal. Every trip to McDonald's was like a jazzercise class for him. When he was six months old, Aileen could not simply sit him in a high chair and feed him. She would have to have toys and books and a movie going—anything to distract his attention while she slipped a spoon in his mouth. Aileen and John Jr. would go out with a friend of Aileen's and her baby, and Aileen would just marvel as the other baby finished an 8-ounce bottle. To this day, John Jr. cannot sit down at the table and eat a meal; he stands up and paces around the table repeatedly. He goes on random searches for books, or to check the weather outside. Sometime he just gets up to get up—and then forgets where he wanted to go. And then the cycle begins again.

John Jr. was prone to such severe ear infections that he had to have tubes put in his ears when he was very young. It affected his balance. He was plenty strong, but when he'd try to walk he'd fall over. If you held his hand, he could walk forever, and even run, but he couldn't take a step alone. But the tubes had begun to work. During the summer of 1996, at Aileen's family reunion, her cousin was running with John Jr., holding his hand. All of a sudden, she kind of stumbled and ac-

accidentally let go of his hand, and John took off running as fast as anyone had ever seen a one-and-a-half-year-old run. His first steps were about a hundred-yard dash, and he hasn't stopped running since.

By the time he was a toddler, we knew that something wasn't quite right with him, in ways very different from his brother and sister. John Jr. exhibited what we later learned is the classic symptom of Attention Deficit Hyperactivity Disorder (ADHD): the sense that he had a "motor" on his back. The energizer bunny on speed. One time a limo driver picked us all up in California and was staring at John Jr. as he bounced around the back of the car and rapid-fired questions as we drove to the hotel. The driver finally asked, "Does he have an off button?"

It went from "global developmental delay" to "sensory integration disorder," and every time some new diagnosis was mentioned, we'd buy another book and read up on it and fret anew. No one ever said the words "autism" or "Asperger's Syndrome"; it was always ADD or ADHD.

By the time he started school, we realized he had a real problem, but we just could not get a straight answer on what to do. And both of us wondered guiltily whether, with the younger two children struggling with life-or-death health issues on a constant basis, perhaps we had neglected John Jr.'s own special needs.

He was enrolled in a special-needs kindergarten with a teacher who was terrific and just loved him—he'd come home with lipstick all over his face! Once she asked us, "Do you ever just want to drink a bottle of wine after spending a day with your son?" We laughed together and she told us, "Look, you need to help this kid. You need to get him on medicine. I don't tell many people this, but this kid needs help and you need to help him help himself. He can't go through life like this." In our litigious society, teachers are so reluctant to offer opinions. Thank goodness this one did.

John Jr. has been on Ritalin since age six, which has helped him a great deal. He used to be out of control and utterly unable to focus. In the beginning, he couldn't swallow the pill, so the doctor told us to stick it in a teaspoon of applesauce. For years now, it's been a family joke to see a kid bouncing off the walls in a gym or at a playground and whisper, "That one could use some applesauce."

Once he was a student, we also became aware that John Jr. was suffering from severe dyslexia as well, a trait he shares with Aileen. He has come to realize that he's different in many ways from other children—special and gifted in many ways, but different. He's very curious about why that is and asks a bevy of questions about it. We tell him, "You know what, John? Yes, you're dyslexic. But so is Tom Cruise. And you have ADHD, but so does President Bush."

John Jr. asks questions about everything. It can be trying at times. Long after the other kids grew out of replying "Why?" to every explanation, he was still following up, to the point that speaking with him sometimes feels like a deposition. He'll probably make a great litigator someday. "Mr. Justice Crowley" has a nice ring to it. Meanwhile, obsessive question asking is a signature trait of Asperger's Syndrome, along with poor communication skills, repetitive routines, lack of eye contact, and physical clumsiness. Asperger's may turn out to be the final, most apt diagnosis of John Jr.'s uniqueness.

You try to keep kids as normal as you can. We signed him up for a T-ball league. You put the ball on the tee, you hit it, and you run. John Jr. was no better or worse than the rest of the kids, but he was always bored and disinterested. I remember going to the games and seeing him out there and feeling proud of my son in his little uniform. By this point, Megan and Patrick were on their ventilators and I thought, hey, at least John will be my baseball star in the family.

So in this one game, John hits the ball very hard and gets all the way to second base. The next kid hits a double, too, and we cheer, "Go, John, go!" We didn't notice that while he was standing on second base, John Jr. got bored; there was apparently not enough action going on in the game for his liking. To pass the time, he decided it would be an awesome idea to take the bag off the post that's pounded into the dirt. For good measure, he also kicked dirt into the hole, so the coaches couldn't return it to its correct position. Now it's all crooked and off-kilter, and the game has to stop while the coaches go to the concession stand for plastic spoons to try to re-dig the hole. Aileen is great about this stuff, but I get—or at least used to get—very self-conscious and feel the stares of other parents. This was especially so in the days when Megan and Patrick were just starting down the path of perpetual stares.

So the game continues and eventually John is on defense, playing the infield. Once again, he gets bored and the next thing we know the umpire yells, "No!!!" and practically dives for John, who once again has taken the bag out of the ground. Later in that same game, while he's on second base he keeps trying to get the attention of the kid playing shortstop. I keep trying to stage-whisper, "Pay attention! Watch the batter!" But John Jr. keeps saying "psst" to the shortstop. Finally, he simply picks up a handful of dirt and throws it in the kid's face. The shortstop, a head taller than John Jr., is about to pummel him when all the parents run out to break it up.

John is not a bad kid at all. In fact, he is one of the most warmhearted and kind kids you could ever meet. He had no idea why everyone was so upset. He was just trying to create some action.

That was the end of team sports for John Jr. His doctor told us—arguably, a bit too late—that kids with severe ADHD don't do well in team sports. He is now running track and doing well at it. He runs the hundred-yard dash. For longer races, he loses interest and just kind of stops.

When Megan was about nine years old, John Jr. was running around the house like a maniac with a yellow bucket on his head. He apparently thought that the bucket would act as both skull protectant and symbol of masculine power. Megan just looked at me and said, "I'll tell you what, Dad—I know I need one enzyme to get me all better. I have absolutely no idea how many enzymes your company needs to make for John."

Some predict the world will end on the day the Mayan calendar ends: December 21, 2012. December 21 is John Jr.'s birthday. That year he will turn eighteen. It's amazing that the Mayans had such prophetic abilities to foresee that the end of days would come on the exact day that the State of New Jersey grants John Jr. his full driver's license.

John Jr. struggles with focus. He has a very difficult time having conversations, and even Aileen and I often cannot get him to look us in the eye when he speaks. It's made it very difficult for him to make friends. The boys will go outside to run through the woods and play war and other games, and John Jr. can't do that. He can't pretend or see the world through others' perspective, which is another classic symptom on the autism spectrum. Where Megan can sit all day playing with her Barbie and making up stories, he requires concrete facts.

John Jr.'s inability to form friendships with his peers has been painful at times to watch. One night, I went into his room and, as usual, he was poring over a big book. I looked a little more closely and saw that it was actually two big books: his copy of the middle school yearbook and Megan's copy. He was comparing them page by page to see if there were any differences, even though they were the same book. Finally, he got to the rear pages, where kids sign each other's books. One of the books had a ton of signatures and the other had only a few. Frankly, I was relieved that John had managed to collect even the handful I saw. I said, "Hey, buddy, you've got some nice autographs there." He replied utterly matter-of-factly, "No, these are all for Megan. When her yearbook ran out of room, her friends wrote to her on mine."

As a parent, your instinct when something like that happens is to sweep your kid into your arms and hug him and tell him it's okay. But John Jr. is never upset by things like this. We ask him all the time, "Are you happy in school? Are kids ever mean to you?" "Yeah, I'm happy," he'll say. And he is. He's just different.

On the other hand, he has a remarkable, almost savant-like long-term memory. He remembers events and places from his first few years of age. John has a room full of history and science books, as well as the *Almanac, The Guinness Book of World Records,* and the *Book of Lists.* He absorbs them all, and his mind is so nimble and interesting that he makes the kind of startling connections that are just a pleasure to behold.

A few years ago, I was trading in my car and the fellow at the dealership asked me for my license plate number on the trade-in. I began to tell him I'd have to go out to the car to look at it, when all of a sudden John Jr. told me the plate number. I asked him how he knew it, and he replied that he knew the license plate numbers of all the cars at our house. Between Aileen and me and the handicapped vans and the nurses' cars, there are typically six or seven cars in our driveway at any given time. He rattled off the license plates of every one of them.

Another time, I took him along to the movies with my buddies Dirk and Brad and a few other guys. He thought it was pretty cool going out with the boys to see the new *Star Trek* movie. I grew up with *Star Trek* in a lot of different iterations, but this was John Jr.'s first exposure to it. Afterward, we went out to dinner at Friday's and John suddenly said, "Dad, has *Star Trek* been around before?" I said, "Yes, John, it has. In fact, over your shoulder there's a picture of a couple of guys named Leonard Nimoy and William Shatner," and I pointed to a photo of the pair, which was hanging on the wall behind him.

I told him that back in the 1960s, it had been a TV show, which was later made into a series of movies, with the first set coming out sometime in the 1980s.

"Oh, like *The Wrath of Kahn*," he said.

"Exactly, John. I think that was the second one. It came out around 1985," I explained.

"No, it was 1982," he claimed.

"Two minutes ago, you didn't even know the movie existed. Now you're telling me when it came out? I'm pretty sure it was 1985, when I was a senior in high school." He insisted on 1982 and lunged for my iPhone so he could look it up on the Internet.

Turns out he was exactly right. When I asked him how on earth he knew that when he didn't even know what *Star Trek* was, he told us that he had seen the last minute of *The Wrath of Kahn* about a year earlier while waiting for some other movie to start, and that he likes to read the tiny print at the end of the credits. We were dumbstruck. Finally, Dirk said, "Nothing like going to dinner with Rain Man."

And it really is like that. John Jr. will rattle off a dozen fascinating facts about an obscure subject someone mentions at the breakfast table. Five minutes later, it'll be time to go to school and he won't be able to find his shoes.

So as different as Megan and Patrick are, John Jr. is different, too. We've come to appreciate those differences in the exact way I hope others appreciate the three of them. When someone doesn't know John well, they think he's just quiet but normal. Once they get to know him, they see that he is a unique character. He can do things other kids can't. We never pity any of our kids and we never let them feel sorry for themselves. We require that they do anything and everything they can to the best of their abilities.

So I don't feel sorry for Aileen and myself when I realize that John is never going to be captain of the baseball team or go to Harvard Law School. He is a special kid with a lot of gifts, and at this point he may still have a world of opportunities open to him. He may never live wholly independently; it might not be safe. But he may well end up being a lot more normal than it seems at this point. In any event, all we want is for him to be happy and to work as hard as he can to be the best person he can be.

Meanwhile, we're very close. Now that he's getting older and we can travel, we've been spending special time together, as I mentioned: heading to Washington, D.C., to look at the monuments or to Notre Dame for a football game. And every couple of days, I drive him to school, which is our special time together. It's a quiet time in the morning for John to get grounded, get his game face on, and he goes from being a little goofball at breakfast to calm and ready for the day at school. When he is ready to leave the car, I tell him each time, "John, I love you. And...'do right....'"—he always quickly finishes my sentence—"... and fear no man.' I know. I love you, too, Dad." He looks at me the best he can, smiles, and heads out to face the world in his own special way.

Neither Megan nor Patrick has ever been out of earshot of an adult. Independence is a major issue for them, and it's critical to allow them to make decisions and afford them some modicum of self-determination. Like all parents, we struggle with the instinct to protect them from all possible harm or disappointment versus the desire to allow them to grow up and take chances.

Megan prizes her ability to get around on her own, courtesy of her motorized wheelchair. Her personality is such that she worries very little whether a particular doorframe was built to accommodate her 300-pound steel go-cart. If she doesn't quite fit, too bad for the doorframe. When Megan's chair needs an occasional twenty-four-hour repair, her nurse has to push her around school instead of simply walking behind her. This drives Megan crazy, and you can really see how much it means to her to control this little bit of her world.

When we were moving to our current house in 2002, we were all thrilled to be entering a home that we'd designed to be as accessible as possible, with wide doorways and plenty of ramps. Megan had experienced a tremendous rush of freedom and growth when we first got her a motorized wheelchair a couple of years earlier. Aileen thought that the new house presented an opportunity to get one for Patrick, too.

I wasn't so sure. Patrick wasn't quite as strong or coordinated as Megan, and he was nowhere near as confident (few are, actually). Aileen insisted, and she is so intuitive about when to challenge the kids and push them to achieve. We bought the chair and equipped it and explained to Patrick how it works.

On the day after the move, I called home from work to ask how things were going in the new house. Aileen said, "Wait till you see Patrick. He's zooming all over the kitchen." I smiled and was glad to have been wrong, thinking about my sweet and shy son—every bit as introverted as Megan is extroverted—suddenly getting a modicum of independence.

I came home that evening and there were boxes all over the place as Aileen pulled the house together. She had all the kitchen cabinets open because we were putting away our plates. I saw Patrick in his new wheel-chair and said, "Hey, buddy, look at you!" He wanted to come greet me, but as he turned to do so, he lost control of the chair and went flying through the kitch-en, knocking every single cabinet door off its hinges. Aside from having to replace the cabinet doors, we re-alized the chair wasn't safe for Patrick. And it really scared him. A motorized wheelchair turned out not to be a good fit for Patrick, and that's fine. But we don't let such setbacks turn into defeats.

The whole family went to Portland to visit the set while the movie about us was being filmed. It's not that easy to get the kids to school. Getting them across the country is another story. Flying on a commercial flight is out of the question. The kids cannot sit upright for that long. But even chartering a private jet creates chal-lenges. For one thing, each wheelchair weighs about 300 pounds—it's not like Aileen and I can just toss it up the stairs. For another, the pressure changes af-fect their respirators, so we have to be even more alert to the warning buzzers on their respirators. And then there's arranging for appropriate handicapped vans on the other side of the trip, as well as accommodations that can handle the equipment and wheelchairs. The Crowley Fun Machine on cross-country trips is like a mobile MASH unit.

When we landed in Portland, Megan's wheel-chair's motor would not function. As I struggled on the tarmac to disassemble the electrical system,

I thought of the gap between our real lives and the glamour of a Hollywood movie. I was lying on the pavement in shorts and a T-shirt in the pouring rain struggling to fix her chair—and I'm not exactly known as a "MacGyver" around the house. After I finally got the wheelchair moving, I went back into the plane to carry Megan down the stairs. I told her, "Megan, you put the 'high' in 'high maintenance.'" She replied, "Daddy, if we were a normal family coming off a normal plane, why would they ever make a movie of us?" She had a point.

Any family would find it thrilling, and surreal, to see themselves portrayed by well-known actors. It was the starkest possible reminder that our family is indeed different. And that those differences, which on any given day can easily seem like insurmountable hurdles, are actually wonderful reasons to celebrate, gifts from God to be appreciated and treasured.

Those differences were in full relief during the shooting of the movie. I've already discussed John Jr.'s shyness and trouble making eye contact. Another element to his social awkwardness is that he doesn't have a filter; if he has a thought, he just says it. (I constantly remind him, "Inside voice, outside voice.")

On our first day on the soundstage, we were all elated to be there. We were having fun taking pictures with Harrison Ford and Brendan Fraser and Keri Russell and the rest of the cast and Tom Vaughn and all of the crew. The boy who was playing John Jr. was a ten-year-old from Louisville, Kentucky, named Sam Hall.

Like all these child actors, Sam was incredibly precocious, and he and his family also happened to be very thoughtful.

The Hall family brought gifts for my kids. Being from Louisville, they gave Megan a miniature pink bat with her name inscribed on it. Then Sam presented John with a full-size major-league Louisville Slugger engraved with his name. Sam handed it to John, with the film crew and Harrison Ford standing there, and said, "John, I'm honored to be playing you in this movie. Here's a special bat to thank you for this honor." John took the bat, looked at it, and announced, "I already have a bat like this, thank you," and handed it back! Aileen and I just cringed. I whispered to him, "Take the damn bat!" John Jr. replied, totally oblivious, "But, Dad, I already have one."

Actually, the fun began before we even arrived in Portland.

Megan was *very* concerned about who would be cast to play her. When the movie was being discussed, the first actress they talked about was Dakota Fanning. But by the time the studio was ready to start shooting, Ms. Fanning would have been too old to play Megan during the time in which *Extraordinary Measures* takes place. The producers then came very close to working with Abigail Breslin, who had played the title character in *Little Miss Sunshine*. Megan raised her eyebrows. She hadn't heard of Abigail and wanted to be sure whoever was portraying her would have the range and chops to convey her every nuance. Not to mention marquee appeal. I told Megan that Abigail Breslin had received an Oscar nomination as a nine-year-old. Megan suggested that Miley Cyrus was more like what she had in mind, and even brought up Cameron Diaz.

So we rented *Little Miss Sunshine* and Aileen said, "There's absolutely no way Megan is seeing this." I offered to fast-forward all the naughty parts and Aileen approved, with me adding, "Come on, it's a little girl, how bad can it be?" So Megan and I watched it. At first, Megan was very skeptical, and didn't like the girl but was really into the movie. By the time we got to the end, with the faux striptease to "Superfreak," Megan was clapping and kind of doing the dance with her arm, singing along. Megan concluded, "This girl is perfect. She would do a great job as me."

As it happens, Abigail Breslin also grew too old to play Megan at eight years old. The director, Tom Vaughan, first came to visit us in the summer of 2007, and he got to know Megan a bit. Then he came back a year later and spent a good deal of time with our family. That's when he came to understand what a vivid character Megan is and the profound influence she has on everyone she meets: her indomitable spirit, going all the way back to when she refused to die in the hospital, her eyes burning with defiance against the fading of the light.

Tom thought it through and said, "We've got to change the screenplay. We've really got to build up Megan as a character." So they went back and edited and rewrote sections of the screenplay with the screen-writer, Bob Jacobs, to beef up Megan's role. They had Harrison Ford, who had originally optioned the idea to co-star as a scientist in the movie. They said find-ing someone to play me and Aileen would be relative-ly straightforward, but they believed casting Megan would be the toughest challenge. By the fall of 2008 they began the process of selecting a young actress to play Megan. They wanted a newcomer and put out a casting call nationwide.

And we knew they were doing that, but we were busy, we hadn't kept in touch, and then Aileen's cous-in called in the fall to say, "You guys have to go on YouTube and just type in Megan Crowley and see what comes up."

Apparently, what they do is put out to all these talent agencies and theater groups around the coun-try a description of the role and say, "If interested, send us your DVD." Two thousand kids sent in audi-tions portraying one page of the screenplay. Aileen and I went on YouTube and saw about twenty young girls who had posted their audition to play Megan in the "Untitled Crowley Project." Some of them were shockingly good and others were very amateurish. But just watching these young girls say, "Hi, I'm Megan Crowley" was surreal. When Megan saw the clips, her first reaction was, "Gosh, this is so odd." And then almost immediately, she turned movie critic and concluded, "These girls aren't good enough."

In January, the producers called to tell us they had found their Megan: a remarkable eight-year-old named Meredith Droeger, who had auditioned in Chicago. A few weeks later, Aileen and I flew to California and they showed us a screen test. On the DVD they played for us, we heard the director's voice and then Harrison Ford's voice. Harrison and Meredith acted out a scene for five minutes or so, and we just knew—this was Megan.

Meredith is not a cutesy Hollywood type. She's a tough, smart, precocious little kid. There's a sweet moment at the end of her screen test when you hear Tom Vaughn's voice.

"Well, Meredith, how do you think you did?" he asks.

She's a little kid, sitting on her hands, and replies, "I don't know. I think I did okay."

"We think you did really well," he says. "Do you know who that actor was who was acting with you?"

She shrugs her shoulders and says, "I don't have any idea."

"Do you like *Star Wars?*" Tom asks.

"Not really," she says.

"Well, how about *Indiana Jones?*" he tries.

"Oh, I love *Indiana Jones!*" she cries. "I just saw the last one."

Tom starts to tell her that the fellow she was just acting with is none other than Indiana Jones when Meredith's eyes get big and she looks off camera toward her mom and dad and says, "No way! You know what? They kind of look alike."

When we showed the DVD to Megan and asked her what she thought, even she agreed that "she's good enough to play me."

I have a wonderful photo of Megan looking at the screen as they showed us some of the dailies, which are the rough cuts of the prior week's shootings. The sheer intensity on Megan's face watching herself being portrayed was something I'll never forget. The girls wound up being very nice friends, even though Megan is four years older. We were getting ready to leave after our week there, and Megan by that point had gotten comfortable watching Meredith in the wheelchair playing her. Just as we were about to go, Megan said, "I want to say goodbye to Meredith."

We were on this huge 100,000-square-foot soundstage. I said, "All right, Megs, let's go find her." Meredith was in one of the buildings they had built on the soundstage to re-create a bedroom at our beach house. She was rehearsing with Brendan Fraser, and I mentioned to her that Megan and the rest of the family were about to head back home. She jumped out of the wheelchair and said, "Megan is leaving?" Even though I'd seen it a hundred times after a week of filming, it still gave me a tiny jolt to see "Megan" or "Patrick" suddenly stand up out of their wheelchairs.

Meredith started running toward Megan, and realized she had bare feet and the floor was dirty and covered with wires and movie stuff. She looked up at me, and I said, "I'll carry you, sweetie." So I carried her over and plopped her down right next to Megs. I said, "Meredith, Megan has to go home now and she just wanted to say goodbye." Megan looked at her and said, "Bye. I'll write to you." Meredith said, "I'll write, too, and maybe I'll come visit this summer."

And then there was silence; they didn't know what to say. It was like kids leaving summer camp—they don't want to say goodbye. And Megan looked at Meredith and kind of awkwardly reached over and put her hand on Meredith's shoulder and said, "I'm really proud that you're playing me in the movie." Meredith looked at Megan and said, "I'm really proud to be playing you, Megan." They gave each other a hug and they each went off in different directions. Neither of them had tears in their eyes. Only I did.

ACKNOWLEDGMENTS

This book is about strength, hope, and joy. The people I thank here have provided strength, hope, and joy throughout our lives. We've been blessed to have hundreds of family, friends, teachers, mentors, colleagues, partners, priests, commanding officers, and even competitors, all of whom helped develop our ideas and elevate our souls.

Our first debt is one of gratitude and it is owed to our families: Aileen's parents, Marty and Kathy, and John's mother, Barbara, and stepfather, Lou, our brothers and in-laws, Brian, Kim, Marty, Joseph, and Jason, John's grandmother Jeanette, Aunt Michele, Uncle Jimmy and Aunt Marie, and Aunt Cappi and Uncle Carlo, Aileen's Uncle Charles, Aunt Jane, Aunt Sandra and Uncle Jim, as well as scores of Irish and Italian cousins with the last names of Crowley, Holleran, O'Dea, Jordan, Beneventano, Buonacorsi, Budicini, Ranes, Reilly, and Ruddy. (Sounds like roll call at a New York City Fire Station, I know.) And, of course, the Janeskis (some Polish relatives made it proudly onto the family tree!). And John's dad, Sgt. John F. Crowley, Englewood Police Department, may he continue to rest in peace now as he has since John and Joseph were very young boys.

Acknowledgments

From elementary school through law school, many of our teachers and classmates left a lasting impression. The devoted instructors at Bergen Catholic High School, Georgetown University, the U.S. Naval Academy, Trinity College, Notre Dame Law School, and Harvard Business School all helped nurture our love of learning. This book would not have been possible without the efforts of those who believed in it from the beginning. Esther Margolis, Harry Burton, Heidi Sachner, Skye Senterfeit, Haley Pierson, Paul Sugarman, and Keith Hollaman at Newmarket Press gave new meaning to the phrase "crash schedule." Our publicists, Christina Papadopoulos and Raina Seides at BWR, labored tirelessly to ensure that people heard our story. Phillipa Brophy at Sterling Lord earned her reputation for never taking no for an answer. Our friend Andrea Spalla was so very helpful in reviewing an early draft of this book and sharing her candid views and thoughts.

We have been joined in various business pursuits in biotechnology by many wonderful people, each of whom has contributed to the ongoing quest for a treatment for Pompe disease over the past decade, each in a different way: Bradley Campbell, Tony McKinney, Julie Smith, William Canfield, Henri Termeer, Jan van Heek, David Lockhart, Matt Patterson, Pol Boudes, Nicole Schaeffer, Geoff Gilmore, Jim Dentzer, Brian Markison, Myrtle Potter, Hung Do, Bill Fallon, Pedro Huertas, Gus Lawlor, Dennis Purcell, Steve Elms, Josh

Phillips, Sherrill Neff, Steve Roth, Dave Alberts, Mike Raab, and Doug Branch.

We are blessed with many terrific friends. Naming them would take a book unto itself. An incomplete list includes the Devinneys, the Macfarlanes, the Spadeas, the Palazs, the Ostergards, the Gordons, the Sewells, the Poissons, the Zides, the Ivancichs, the Davises, the Westdyks, and the Mitchells.

Without the dedication and passion of Geeta Anand, a Pulitzer Prize–winning writer with the *Wall Street Journal*, our journey might never have been told in newspaper or in book. I thank the actors, writers, and tech people who helped tell our family's story so movingly in *Extraordinary Measures*: Harrison Ford, Brendan Fraser, Keri Russell, and the rest of the cast, and director Tom Vaughan and screenwriter Bob Jacobs. Special thanks to Michael Shamberg, Carla Santos Shamberg, and Stacy Sher, the producers of the film at Double Feature Films. Years ago, we entrusted our life story to them. They could not have handled it with more care and devotion. Thanks, too, to Amy Baer and her terrific team at CBS films for bringing this story to the big screen.

Our children's lives have been preserved and enhanced by superb health care professionals. Sharon Dozier, our larger-than-life Arkansas Florence Nightingale, is a part of our family, as are her children, her husband, Eddie, and her grandchildren. Our kids owe much of their life to her loving care. Other wonderful nurses and therapists include Yvonne Holloway,

Acknowledgments

Marek and Kathy Cieply, Maryanne Naro, Maryellen Allen, Marian Marcario, Carol Knigge, Anne Jacobs, Lynne Bridge, Marylou Brown, and literally scores of others who have helped us with the kids over the years, along with Drs. Y. T. Chen, Barry Byrne, Alfred Slonim, Debra Day-Salvatore, Valerie Kullman, Marc Hofley, Yitzak Schnapps, and Michael Tavil.

Ken Kurson helped write this book. His gifted prose, organization, dedication, and commitment to this project made it what it is. *Chasing Miracles* would not have come to be if it were not for Ken. He is a great writer, a thoughtful friend, and a fierce partner. Ken would like to thank his lovely wife, Rebecca, a true woman of valor, and their three delicious kids, Steve, Carrie, and Chaya. He would also like to thank his mother, Annette Kurson, for teaching him how to write, his father, Jack Kurson z'l, for teaching him how to tell a story, his brother, Robert Kurson, for being the best writer in America, and his sister, Jane Glover, for being the best listener he knows. He also thanks Larry Weitzner and everyone at Jamestown Associates for their patience and his best friends, Kevin Sanders and John Packel, for their unending support.

Finally, we want to thank our three children, John Jr., Megan, and Patrick. Read the dedication of this book and you'll know why.